Praise for Malcolm Mahr's

Murder at the Paradise Spa

"*Murder at the Paradise Spa* will take you on a fun-filled yet sympathetic and highly informative romp through Haitian art, religion and culture."

—Joseph R. L. Stern,
former Editorial Page Editor,
The Baltimore Sun

"High praise for *Murder at the Paradise Spa*, on behalf of the entire community of the Haitian people."

—Max Beauvoir,
Voodoo priest and Ati-Houngan,
Temple of Yehwe

"Mr. Mahr's novel is the revalorization of a culture and religion that too long has been demonized. It's definitely a must read."

—Marleine Bastien,
Ms. Magazine's "Woman of the Year"

"Has a zany slant that makes it intriguing as a mystery. Most unusual and great fun."

—Muriel Dobbin,
McClatchy Newspapers

"This fun novel provides a quick and painless education in Haitian Voodoo art."

—Selden Rodman, Author,
The Miracle of Haitian Art; Where Art is Joy

Murder
at the
Paradise Spa

Malcolm Mahr

Fiction Publishing, Inc.
5626 Travelers Way
Ft. Pierce, Florida 34982

ISBN: 978-0-9825086-3-3

Previously published as *Don't Feed Peanuts to a Zombie*

Printed in the United States of America

For Fran, of course.

Farim bon ki ra.

Also by Malcolm Mahr

FICTION

The Secret Diary of Marco Polo

The Mystery of DaVinci's Monna Vanna

NONFICTION

How to Win in the Yellow Pages

What Makes a Marriage Work

You're Retired Now. Relax.

Acknowledgments

THIS NOVEL IS A WORK OF FICTION. It is, however, based to some extent on true facts and serious events.

Haitian art collectors are a remarkably cooperative group of men and women who generously afforded me the privilege of including their artwork. I would particularly like to thank Ned Hopkins, James Fastenrath, Dr. Rudolf H. Boulos, Carol Cleaver, Ute Stebich, Astrid and Halvor Jaeger, and the Yale University Art Gallery.

Special thanks to Max Beauvoir, houngan of the Temple of Yehwe, Washington, D.C., for his wisdom, guidance, and words of advice: "If you're going to do it—do it right." I hope I have.

"A world without spirits is a wasteland."

—*Joseph Campbell*

PART I

THE ZOMBIE

I am the scorn of my adversaries,
a horror to my neighbors.
an object of dread to my acquaintances;
those who see me in the street flee from me.

—Psalm 31:11-13

...1

THE DAY BERNARD GUZMAN BECAME A ZOMBIE dawned blood red over the Atlantic. Rapidly advancing thunder boomed and echoed across the darkening water. Charcoal-colored stratus clouds were illuminated by crackling bursts of forked lightning. The wind hissed wildly among the newly-planted coconut palms lining route A1A, snapping off small branches. Residents of Hutchinson Island awoke to earsplitting thunder clapping directly over their heads.

In nearby Fort Pierce, a Haitian woman slammed her storm shutters closed as heavy rain pelted against her windows. She crossed herself and muttered in Creole, "*Le ou we Danto pase, ou di se loray-o.* When red-eyed Erzulie Danto be mad, somebody gon' die."

"FROM FORT PIERCE, FLORIDA," the CNN anchorman announced with a thin smile, "we have fast-breaking news of an *alleged* zombie on the loose. We go live to our reporter, Marilyn Lamont, who is at the scene."

"On this scenic island on the beautiful Treasure Coast of Florida," Lamont said, "police are investigating the reported sighting of a man believed to be a zombie." In the background a cluster of elderly, white-haired people waved at the cameras. The CNN reporter continued, "The alleged zombie is believed to be Bernard L. Guzman, age 67, president of the OceanHouse Condominium Association on Hutchinson Island. The information CNN has received is that Guzman collapsed last week from unknown causes. He was discovered in a coma by a cleaning lady who called 911. The man was rushed to a local emergency room." She rifled her notes. "At Lawnwood Regional Medical Center here in Fort Pierce, doctors pronounced Bernard Guzman dead on arrival."

The anchorman interrupted, "We have by phone at his home in

Cap-Haïtien, Haiti, a leading authority on the subject of zombies, Dr. Roger Ducasse. He is the author of the well-reviewed *Zombie Monologues*. What is your take on the situation in Fort Pierce, doctor?"

"It is a pleasure to be on your program," Ducasse said. "Zombies are mythical creatures believed to appear as reanimated corpses or mindless human beings mysteriously rising from their grave." He chuckled. "The zombie fantasies originated in the Afro-Caribbean spiritual belief system called Voodoo, which told of people being controlled as laborers by a powerful sorcerer—"

"Bottom line, doctor," the CNN man interrupted. "Would I be correct to say you do not believe in the existence of zombies, or the living dead?"

"The living dead is a Haitian peasant superstition that unfortunately gained prominence in your Hollywood horror films. Death is not merely the loss of bodily function; it is the material decay of the cells and tissue. One does not wake up the dead. In psychiatric terms, people who are called 'zombies' more than likely are suffering from catatonic schizophrenic, a condition characterized by incoherence, stupor and mindlessness—"

"Thank you, Dr. Ducasse," the anchor cut in again. "Back to Marilyn for a wrap-up."

"Ray, burial services were held on Friday, and Mr. Guzman was laid to what was supposed to be his final rest at a local cemetery. Two days later," she added, "the deceased man was sighted by a fellow resident of the OceanHouse Condominium, a Dr. Maxwell Wolfe.

"According to a statement by Dr. Wolfe, who is a retired psychologist from Johns Hopkins in Baltimore, on Sunday morning he was playing golf at the Fairwinds Golf Course off of US1. Dr. Wolfe claimed that he saw a bald man stumbling across the green on the difficult five-par, dogleg 14th hole. The person's face was pale and blank, but Wolfe recognized his presumably deceased neighbor because of the green and yellow plaid madras shorts with the high black socks that Guzman always wore. The doctor yelled to the man, but he ran off."

"A bald zombie wearing green and yellow madras shorts with high black socks," the anchor echoed. "Can you picture that?" He was trying to keep from breaking up on camera.

Marilyn Lamont continued, "After the news of Bernard Guzman's eerie reappearance was reported on local news, the Ocean-House Women's Committee requested that the grave be reopened. The ladies needed to know for certain whether their condo president was *de facto* dead. If so, they intended to go ahead and re-cover the lobby furniture.

"I have with me Wanda Smeltzer, chairperson of the Ocean-House Condominium Women's Committee. Would you care to comment on the situation?"

"We are naturally upset about poor Bernard," Wanda Smeltzer said. "It's a damn shame, but life goes on, and the furniture in the lobby is a disgrace."

The screen shifted back to the CNN studio. "And did authorities reopen the grave?"

"Yes, Ray, this morning both the coroner's office and the Fort Pierce police officiated while Bernard Guzman's grave was dug up and the heavy casket reopened—it was empty."

...2

"WHAT AILS, Bernie?" Maxwell Wolfe had inquired of the condominium president a week prior, when Guzman telephoned late at night in a panic. Wolfe was a broad-shouldered man in his early eighties with white hair, prominent features, and perceptive blue eyes that seemed to take in Guzman with skepticism and a trace of grim amusement, as if to say, *What have I gotten into?*

"I can't sleep," Guzman whined. "A nightmare wakes me every night. It's driving me nuts. You were a shrink," he said. "Help me. I'm desperate."

Wolfe looked at the bald condominium president sprawled on a white leather sofa. Guzman had a dazed look on his face. With stubby hands, his neighbor clutched an ice pack to his forehead.

"Psychotherapy isn't like calling a plumber to unplug your disposal. I'm retired. If you want help, I'll get references for you to call. Have you tried sleeping pills?"

Guzman started to answer, then paused as though he'd lost the thread.

Wolfe sat down, looked around and waited, preferring to give Guzman space to begin explaining his problem without rushing in with questions or trying to put him too much at ease. His neighbor's taste in art surprised him. Colorful paintings hung floor to ceiling against white stuccoed walls. To Wolfe the artwork looked two-dimensional, almost childlike, in raw colors: a bearded man on a horse; people dressed in white sheets in a graveyard; and in the center of the room, prominently lit, a painting of a dark-skinned nude woman standing amid vibrant multicolored flowers and birds.

Guzman broke the silence. "At first, I thought it was a crazy nightmare. But the same weird dream kept coming back, haunting me: a half-naked woman with her back to me, smoking a cigarette and sitting on the lap of a giant owl. It seemed so real; a terrifying creature with talons as big as the paws of a fucking mountain lion. The demon just stares at me—"

"That *is* a foreboding dream, Bernard. Ordinarily, I wouldn't consider providing therapeutic first aid. I don't even have a Florida license. But you're my neighbor, and obviously in psychic pain. Frequently a first dream episode is important to talk about while it's still fresh in your mind. Freud introduced the importance of the first dream interpretation, and many of my colleagues believe the initial dream— or in your case, a horrific nightmare—could represent the translation into dream language of the content of one's neurosis. So it might be beneficial for you to talk about your dream. What's the first thing you think of when the nightmare awakens you?"

Guzman ran his hands over his sweating scalp and frowned. "Haiti. That damn owl reminds me of Haiti."

"Haiti?" Wolfe repeated, lifting his eyebrows in surprise.

"My father had a pharmaceutical company in Port-au-Prince. After he died, I ran it." Wolfe remained silent, waiting for Guzman to continue. "In Haiti, I met a girl. Her mother was a *mambo*—"

"A what?"

"A Voodoo priestess. The old woman taught me the roots that cured river blindness."

"Onchocerciasis?"

"Yeah. I had the roots analyzed by a lab, then took out a patent. I named it Ivermectin."

Wolfe couldn't keep the tone of annoyance out of his voice. "You stole the formula?"

"Spare me your moral judgment. I learned from my old man that if you want something in this world—women, money, anything —you can't worry about who gets hurt. He taught me that there were only winners and losers. I wasn't going to be a loser."

"Not the perfect role model," Wolfe said, the edge still there.

"My father went to the University of Michigan. He met a fellow student, François Duvalier. They became buddies. Duvalier was a Haitian physician specializing in the treatment of a tropical disease— yaws."

Wolfe nodded. "I know about yaws. Natives of the Caribbean

injured themselves cutting sugar cane, and the cuts became infected and—"

Guzman interrupted, "Yeah. Well, Duvalier was taking graduate courses in public health at Michigan. That's how they hooked up. Years later, when my father was in the pharmaceutical business, he produced a batch of substandard penicillin that didn't meet FDA standards. Pop contacted his old Haitian buddy and sold the penicillin to Duvalier. The penicillin was at first administered with beeswax in oil; two injections at a ten-to-twelve-hour interval. Later, Dad made Duvalier a cheaper penicillin preparation that with one intramuscular injection was effective against endemic treponematoses. It helped cure yaws and made Duvalier famous. Haitians called him Papa Doc. In 1957 my parents moved to Port-au-Prince. That was the year Duvalier became president."

"Why does Haiti come to mind in your dreams?"

"That Duvalier was one scary bastard to do business with, always wearing dark glasses and dressed in black. And after he went into politics, he never paid his bills for our penicillin. After he became president, he recruited an army of thugs, Tonton Macoutes, for his personal bodyguards. Everybody in Haiti feared Duvalier because on his whim, they could be arrested and dumped into the place called the dungeon of death, Fort Dimanche."

Wolfe nodded, steepled his hands and remained silent.

"Fort Dimanche was run by a woman. The superstitious natives believed she was a *loup garou*, a Haitian werewolf." He shrugged. "You wouldn't understand. It's a Voodoo thing."

Wolfe smiled. "I don't believe in witchcraft, vampires, werewolves, demons, UFO's, astrology or any of that new-wave mumbo-jumbo. But then, I didn't grow up in Haiti. Let's talk about the half-naked Haitian woman in your dreams."

The condo president sat in stony silence.

"You're the one who called me for help, Bernard. Remember? We're on a fast track. Free associating may be a good way to bring your concerns to the surface."

Guzman remained stubbornly mute. He fidgeted on the sofa, showing his impatience.

Wolfe attempted a new tactic. "Where did you find this remarkable artwork?"

"It was my old man's collection. He had a friend in Port-au-Prince, an American named Peters who started a school for a bunch of untrained would-be artists: taxi drivers, gardeners, even some weird Voodoo priests. Peters tutored Dad on which artists to buy from."

Pointing to the framed 2-by-3 foot oil on masonite of the dark-skinned nude woman that Wolfe had admired, Guzman chuckled, "I didn't pay for this one. I stole it from the bogey man himself, Papa Doc Duvalier, to recover some of what he owed me."

Wolfe looked again at the lush painting of the nude woman standing in a forest surrounded by birds in brilliant pastel shades. Two pairs of rose-colored doves flanked her graceful body. The vibrant colors of the flowers complemented the woman's beauty. "To me, art is mostly wallpaper for the rich," he said. "But your collection is impressive. This painting is awesome."

Guzman's phone rang. Mouthing an apology, he walked into the bedroom.

Wolfe eyed a sepia photograph matted and framed in glossy black steel. A young Bernard Guzman's arms encircled the waist of a beautiful dark-skinned girl who looked vaguely familiar. As he bent to have a closer look, Wolfe heard a flutter of movement on the balcony. Looking out, he saw a huge owl staring with unblinking, large, yellow-orange eyes. Its feathers were black, with a brownish sheen; the bird's neck was banded with white. Its beak was black and curved. At rest on the railing with its wings folded back, the creature looked the size of a small bear. He felt an adrenaline rush rising in his throat as the creature snapped its beak, then flew off.

Wolfe heard Guzman arguing with someone called Honey. Then the phone slammed down and the condo president reentered the living room.

"I know this sounds crazy," Wolfe said, "but there was a large owl perched on your deck."

Guzman's eyes narrowed. "You goddammed shrink," he yelled, his sharp face frozen into a mask of hostility. "First you con me into telling you my nightmare with all that Freud bullshit, and then you make fun of it. Get *out* of here and leave me alone!"

Well, I certainly handled that well, Wolfe mused pensively as he waited for the elevator.

"Hello, Dr. Max, dear. I heard shouting."

"All's well," Wolfe replied to Guzman's neighbor, Wanda Smeltzer, observing the skimpy red Japanese kimono that exposed much of her shapely if overripe figure. The vee of Wanda Smeltzer's robe revealed the melon curvature of her breasts.

As he stepped into the elevator, Wolfe said, "It's nice to see you again, Wanda—especially so much of you."

...3

THE WOMAN OPENED THE DOOR A CRACK—the length of the security chain. She studied the man standing there, six-two and thick-bodied. His gray hair was thinning.

"My name is Perini, ma'am," he said in a weary tone. "I'm the Fort Pierce police chief, and I'd like to talk to your husband. Is he at home?"

Millie Wolfe allowed his question to register a moment before asking to see identification, then unlocking the chain and inviting Perini in. She noted the policeman moved with a slow deliberateness that spoke of age, sore muscles and fatigue.

"My husband will be back shortly. He went for the *Times*. Coffee?"

"Thanks, Mrs. Wolfe."

"Millie."

"Thanks, Millie." Perini grinned at the plumpish, good-looking woman fussing over him. "Sorry if I sounded grumpy. I've been up all night. The mayor's worried about round-the-clock talk shows hyping the zombie story to increase their audience ratings. He's afraid the hoopla will scare tourists away from Fort Pierce."

"Did you have breakfast, Chief?"

"No thanks." Perini stifled a yawn. "I'm getting too old for this job."

Millie scoffed, "Men are all the same. My husband didn't know when to quit. Ten years ago, doctors warned Max to slow down, reduce his workload, and lose weight. He ignored them." She sighed. "Within a year he suffered a mild heart attack. I told him that I was going to Florida, and that he could come with me or stay in Baltimore and die. It worked."

"To tell you the truth," Perini said, running his hand through his hair, "I'm fearful of retirement. I don't know what I'd do with myself.

I love fishing, but you can't fish every day, and I don't want to rock away my life in some sorry-assed assisted living facility."

"Is there a woman in your life?"

"Been there, done that. I was working my butt off twenty-four-seven with the Baltimore detective squad. The town was a madhouse. The year I joined, in '68, we had the race riots after Martin Luther King was shot. Then in '78, Baltimore's murder rate was going through the roof because of drugs. All around me, cops were seeing their marriages fall apart. I drank too hard. I put my job ahead of everything—even my kid."

He paused for a pull on his coffee. "It was a sad, familiar story with cops' wives. Mine left me and took my son, Tony. I was a basket case. Then I started reading union vacancy lists. Saw this job offer in Fort Pierce in the detective division, and I took off. Mary was a good woman. She married a corrugated box salesman a year after our divorce."

"*Was* a good woman?"

"Mary died a year ago while my boy was serving in Afghanistan. Her sister called me."

"And your son?"

"Tony and I were tight when he was young," Perini said. "After the divorce, I had to get away from the Baltimore drug scene, the sleazy politicians, my drinking, and the hole in my heart from losing my family. Tony was angry with me. I guess he rightly felt I deserted him. For a few years I sent Christmas and birthday gifts; when he didn't respond, I just let it slide. He sent me an invitation to his West Point graduation, but at the time it was just after the Rodney King thing in California. Avenue D was a powder keg, and Haitian refugees were piling ashore all over Hutchinson Island. I was trying to help them integrate into the community without getting picked up by immigration and shipped back to Haiti. Since then I haven't heard from Tony."

Perini stretched, fidgeted, and glanced at his watch. "I think about the future, but I try not to think too long about it. Maybe I'll get shot in the line of duty and won't have to worry about somebody changing my diapers in a nursing home."

"Nobody goes through life unscathed. More coffee?"

"Thanks, I need the caffeine. How long have you been married?"

"Fifty-five years. We still have screaming matches, but now I turn the fans on so the neighbors don't hear." Millie sighed. "In spite of everything—we still like each other."

"And that's your dirty little secret." Perini grinned. "Do you have kids?"

"One daughter, Natalie Sue. She's married to a hedge fund operator in Palm Beach. He was a friend of that Madoff fellow. Max can't stand Maynard—"

"Tell me about you," Perini asked.

Millie Wolfe reddened. "I used to be a professional singer," she said. "Now, I'm just a fading old nightclub singer with an artificial hip, who can still pack a wallop."

Perini laughed out loud and clapped his hands as he studied the woman's warm, engaging smile. White streaked through her undyed hair, and tiny wrinkles worked their way towards her eyes and mouth, seemingly unchecked by injection or incision.

Encouraged, Millie continued, "And if you'll forgive me for saying it, Chief, in the Fort Pierce area, if you're not young with big tits, forget about getting club gigs anywhere, except in nursing homes."

"What's this about tits?" said Maxwell Wolfe as he came through the back door. "I'm away for ten minutes, and already you're talking dirty and entertaining a stranger in my kitchen."

"Be thankful it's not the bedroom, dear. Meet Captain Perini, the local chief of police."

"I'm running late," Perini said, again glancing at his watch. "Is it okay to ask you a few questions, Dr. Wolfe?"

"Do I need a lawyer?"

"I don't know. Do you?" Perini stared hard, studying Wolfe's eyes, hoping to read something in them. "Mr. Guzman's neighbor, Wanda Smeltzer, said you two had a loud argument the night before he collapsed."

"Wanda is a slut," Millie piped in. "I could tell you plenty about—"

"Excuse me, dear," Wolfe interrupted. "Let me answer the chief's questions."

Perini glanced at his notepad. "Why did Guzman yell 'Get out! Leave me alone!'?"

"Bernie called and asked for my help. He claimed that he was experiencing acute panic attacks caused by reoccurring nightmares about a giant bird that was continually attacking him. I tried a quick-fix because the man was my neighbor. It was unprofessional of me; I should have recommended that he seek counseling from a therapist in the area. Am I a suspect?"

"At this point we have plenty of suspects. Guzman was embezzling from your condo association's reserve funds and preparing to skip town—"

"Embezzling condo funds?" Wolfe interrupted. "I didn't know that."

Perini continued. "We also know that he was having an affair with a married woman employee of the condo management company. She abetted the crime. If he planned to leave her holding the bag, she has motive. The lady's husband also has an age-old reason to do your neighbor harm, and he's in the pest control business, dealing with poisons." The policeman exhaled. "And there's the cleaning lady who found him, a Ms. Beauvoir."

"Josi?" Millie snorted. "That's silly. You really don't think—"

Perini held up his hands. "Folks, everybody is a suspect; this investigation has to be 'by the numbers' because I've got people looking over my shoulder. I double-checked with the doctor at Lawnwood who signed the death certificate. He swears that the guy was dead. He listened for a heartbeat, checked Guzman's breathing—even took his temperature; everything was negative."

"Did they do a brain scan?" Wolfe said.

Perini raised his eyebrows. "No, why?"

"There were some research studies made at Hopkins reviewing cases where a patient was certified as dead and he woke up on a slab in the morgue. It's rare, but it happens."

Perini jotted in his notebook.

Wolfe continued, "It was once conventional wisdom that no

heartbeat proved someone had died. Then they found out that a person's heart could beat so weakly that our instruments couldn't detect it. Did they pump Guzman's stomach?"

Perini nodded. "Fortunately, the contents were saved for autopsy. I sent trace elements to the State Police lab in Orlando. They'll do gas chromatographing."

"What's that?" Millie asked.

The chief said, "They analyze the stomach contents: blood, food, drugs or whatever Guzman ingested. The vapors are then separated and connected to a spectrometer that identifies the substances—and maybe tells us if he was poisoned."

Wolfe nodded approvingly. "I'm impressed."

"I'm glad you're impressed, because I'm confused. To have a homicide, we need a body, and we don't have one. And, for sure, I don't know spit about zombies." He burst out laughing in spite of his puzzlement.

"Haiti is a poor and superstitious country," Wolfe said. "The average Haitian is unfamiliar with catatonic schizophrenia, epilepsy, mental retardation, brain damage or the effects of severe alcoholism. These conditions can produce symptomatic individuals who unknowing people call zombies."

"Well, folks," Perini said, standing up. "I don't know whether we've got a murder, a missing person case or an Elvis sighting. What I do know is that your schizophrenics, alcoholics, epileptics, and people with mental retardation don't crawl out of sealed caskets and wander off."

Perini's cell phone beeped.

"Chief," said Jessie, the police switchboard operator, "that zombie person was sighted on Okeechobee Road, just past the turnpike."

"Who called it in?"

"The lady who runs the Fig Leaf Nudist Park. She said she spotted a creepy-looking bald guy wandering around the grounds in a daze with clothes on. The man had a blank look; she thought he was high on drugs or maybe drunk—"

"Where the hell's the suspect now?" Perini cut in sharply.

"The manager told me that when she confronted him, the guy's eyeballs rotated into the back of his head and his eyes went all white. She screamed and the man skittered off into the scrub pine."

...4

AS THE LAST HONEY-COLORED RAYS of sunlight faded over Lake Okeechobee, the zombie shuffled along dust-choking Florida State Road 70. Passing drivers slowed down and stared curiously at the short, bald, portly white man walking along the highway dressed in mud-splattered yellow and green madras shorts held up by a sisal rope. His tennis shoes were frayed; black socks unraveled around his ankles.

A spine-chilling sound punctured the silence. *Hoo-hoo hooooo hoo-hoo!* The zombie staggered backwards, a bewildered expression on his face at the sight of an enormous owl with tufts of feathers on its head like horns and sharp, deadly talons. The huge raptor perched on the limb of a sixty-foot swamp chestnut tree. It glared down at the zombie. A little shake of breeze ruffled the bird's feathers, revealing large, yellow, piercing eyes with round black pupils. The large owl hissed, its eyes wild, mouth open, teeth bared. It puffed up its feathers, crouching to leap.

In his disoriented state the zombie was confused and frightened. His eyes teared up; his shoulders slumped, and he emitted a muffled cry of despair as the strength ran out of his legs.

A battered pickup truck full of migrant workers rumbled down the dusty highway, kicking up gravel. *"Cómo esta, señor?"* said the driver and crew leader, Juan Martinez. "Would you like to pick oranges, grapefruit—make nice money? We give you food, beer, place to sleep and plenty fucky-fucky. Wha' you say, *amigo?*"

To escape the terrifying owl creature, the zombie managed to scramble aboard.

A shrill sound emanated from the darkness, an ear-piercing screech, like a broken violin with horsehair scraping angrily on catgut. *Whaaa whaaaaaa-a-a-aark.* It was repeated again, chilling, echoing from the brush.

The migrant workers on the truck felt their backbones shiver. The frenzied screech came again. Then the noises stopped completely, and the men exhaled, their stomachs still rigid. In a furious flurry of wings, the huge owl soared away.

...5

THE EBONY-COLORED, LINEBACKER-SIZED MAN took off his dark sunglasses and proffered his picture ID.

"Doesn't the FBI have more important things to do than babysit us?" Perini groused.

The man ignored the barb. "Your office told me I would find you here, Chief."

Wolfe scanned the credentials of Special Agent Preston Dorsett, Federal Bureau of Investigation. He took in the man's appearance: big, well over six feet and broad shouldered. His face was square, with graying black hair just short of a crew cut.

"Let me say something up front," Dorsett said, turning to Perini. "I'm not here to ruffle your feathers. Fort Pierce is your jurisdiction. I'm here as a consultant." He grinned. "In case you haven't noticed, I'm African American, so my FBI superiors, in all of their collective wisdom, figured if it's a zombie, then it must be a black man running wild—send Dorsett."

Perini cracked a tight grin.

Dorsett continued, "Washington is under pressure from your politicos to deep six this zombie business before it becomes a media circus—"

Perini broke in, "They're worried about tourist revenues, and Washington politicians never forget Florida's 27 electoral votes."

"Be that as it may. It's over my pay grade. My day job is agent-in-charge of the Eleventh Department."

"What's the Eleventh Department?" challenged Perini. "Sounds bureaucratic."

"The nation of Haiti is made up of ten geographic zones, called *departments*. Over the years, thousands of Haitians migrated to the U.S. legally." He paused, eyeing Perini. "And as you well know, many illegally. One out of every six Haitians now lives abroad, primarily in this country. For that reason, the Haitian community in the U.S. is called the Eleventh Department."

Wolfe asked, "Shouldn't refugees be an Immigration Service problem, not FBI?"

For a moment the man hesitated. "Good question," he said. "Recently, we've had a rash of murders in the South Miami Haitian community. Local police and the FBI have formed a task force to investigate these crimes that are connected to drug smuggling."

"Do you have a serious drug problem in Miami?" Wolfe asked.

" 'A drug problem.' Makes it sound kind of cute. More like a drug hurricane. Fourteen percent of the cocaine entering the U.S. comes from Haiti, mainly through Florida."

"Why Haiti, and not any other islands in the Caribbean?"

"Traffickers need bases close to the U.S. mainland. Haiti's midway between Colombia and Florida, with 1,500 kilometers of unpatrolled coastline. Most drugs are smuggled on cargo ships. In February, we boarded two Haitian freighters and found twenty million dollars worth of cocaine stashed in hidden compartments below deck covered by fuel oil and slick sludge."

Wolfe studied the fit-looking FBI agent, thinking that the man's eyes were more observant than the leisurely pose he maintained, and that his breezy confidence was artificial.

Dorsett continued. "Then there's the problem of Haitians victimized by paying steep fees to be herded on unsafe boats headed for our waters. We'll never know how many drowned and never made it."

Perini nodded. "We are still picking up Haitian refugees landing on Hutchinson Island."

"Haiti is the poorest country in the hemisphere," Dorsett said. "Average income is less than four hundred dollars a year. Life expectancy is fifty-four. No wonder Haitians seek refuge in the U.S. any way they can. The violence today is reminiscent of Papa Doc Duvalier."

"Duvalier," Wolfe repeated. "Bernard Guzman mentioned his name."

"Papa Doc was a dictator in Haiti in the sixties," Dorsett explained. "He used a paramilitary group of hoodlums, Tonton Macoutes, to do his dirty work. Over sixty thousand Haitians were killed during the twenty-nine-year father-and-son dynasty. Jean-Claude, called Baby Doc, succeeded his father and lived like a king, with a ranch, a mountain retreat, and a beachfront mansion. Jean-Claude now lives in France."

"Guzman told me he had liberated one of Duvalier's paintings," Wolfe said.

Turning to the FBI man, Perini commented, "We're just beginning our investigation. My detectives checked his apartment; nothing appears to be missing."

"Bernie had an extensive Haitian art collection," Wolfe said.

"Chief," Dorsett said. "With your permission, I can ask Professor Louissant, who is the curator of the Bryant Collection of West Indies art at the University of Central Florida, to appraise the Guzman collection."

Perini nodded. "Sure. Why not?"

"Which painting did Mr. Guzman tell you he liberated from Duvalier?" Dorsett asked.

"A dark-skinned, exotic-looking nude woman standing in a bright-colored floral setting."

Perini shook his head, puzzled. "I'm no art expert, but I have thirty years experience examining crime scenes. I can guaran-ass-tee you there was no painting of an exotic-looking black or white nude woman hanging on the wall in Guzman's apartment."

Chief Perini's cell phone rang.

"Boss. We just got a 10-6 call," said the operator. "A huge snake interrupted a robbery-in-progress on 24th Street." She giggled. "It was the perps themselves who called 911."

...6

TWO ASHEN-FACED TEENAGERS huddled together in the back seat of the patrol car that was parked in front of a small house with dark cedar siding.

"What do we have here?" Perini remarked as he rolled down the car window and turned off the air conditioner. He saw a white van marked Florida Wildlife Control parked in the driveway.

The thin, youthful-looking cop said, "Chief, you wouldn't fucking believe it. I answered a 10-6 call and found the front screen door wide open. In a corner of the living room were those two kids holding a cell phone, two small Bose speakers and a Panasonic plasma TV. They're brothers." The officer's eyes widened. "I entered the premises and saw coiled in the middle of the room this huge snake. Jesus. I nearly pissed myself, Chief. Snakes scare me. I'm a city boy."

Perini nodded and stepped out of the car.

"I contacted Florida Wildlife Control, told them it was a police emergency; they sent this guy. You want to talk to him?"

Perini glanced at the wiry wildlife controller. "What's with the reptile?"

The man gave a short, derisive laugh. "Reptile? That snake in there is a twenty-foot African rock python. They are about as big as the giant Burmese pythons, but meaner—so mean they come out of the egg striking. Those babies will prey on pets, small children, hogs, and even alligators."

"That's a fascinating story. You should be on a TV show. Is the *thing* caged?"

The man shook his head. "I wouldn't try to handle a big python like that one without two or three more men, Chief. Your man located the owner. My boss said to hang around until he gets here and make sure nobody gets hurt."

"Are African rock pythons dangerous to adult humans?"

"Word of advice," the wildlife controller said, chuckling. "Don't piss 'em off."

A teal blue 1998 Chevy pickup truck pulled into the parking area. A thin man stepped out wearing khaki pants and a worn blue dungaree shirt, rolled at the cuffs. He had nutmeg skin, a narrow face, short graying hair, and a clipped mustache that drooped at the corners of his mouth. *Haitian,* Perini thought.

"Beauvoir?"

The man fixed Perini with an unblinking gaze. "That's right."

"Using a twenty-foot python as a home security system isn't a good idea," Perini said.

"I believe you will find that I have a valid ROC permit, and since Da is over two inches in diameter, a microchip PIT tag has been implanted as required by Florida law."

"What the hell is an ROC permit?" Perini grumbled.

Beauvoir smiled thinly. "A 'Reptile of Concern' permit," he said. "If you gentlemen will kindly wait outside, I will return Da to his cage."

Perini walked over to the two boys in the police car. He glared at them. The older one said, "I swear to God, sir. I'll never steal again—ever!"

Perini turned to the cop and chuckled. "Whatever it takes to reduce crime in Fort Pierce sounds good to me. Drive the kids home and give them a warning."

The Haitian opened his screen door and motioned the captain inside. Perini cautiously followed Beauvoir into the house as the wildlife controller honked, waved and drove off. The air in the dim living room was still; he sniffed a musky odor. The furnishings looked faded. Shelves of books everywhere. The floor was plain oak strips. No rug. Beauvoir flipped switches and the lights came on. A large five-foot-cube wire cage was positioned in the corner. Inside the cage, Perini noticed a heavy tree branch. Coiling underneath was the largest reptile he had ever seen: a silver-gray python with a triangular head and narrow neck.

Perini glared at Beauvoir long and hard. "Is that cage secure?" he asked, unconsciously sliding a hand towards his holster.

"No worry, Chief. Meet my pet, Da. As you well know, this area has a bad reputation with drugs and crime. When I leave for school, I open Da's cage. He likes to crawl into the sunlight by the window and sleep during the day. At night, he uses the tree branch for climbing."

"What do you feed the thing?"

"Live rats. Da wraps his coils around the rats and squeezes. Instant suffocation."

Perini felt his stomach going acid; he turned away from the cage and spied a tapestry hanging on the wall.

"Interesting wall hanging," Perini said. "Does it have anything to do with your pet?"

"That is a sequined flag portraying Damballah, the supreme snake spirit which was the symbol of the ancient African kingdom of Dahomey, where many Haitian slaves came from. Damballah and Ayida Wedo are the *loa* responsible for bringing the religion of Voodoo from Africa to the Americas. These divinities are envisioned as snakes."

Out of the corner of his eye, Perini rechecked the python.

"According to Haitian myth, the supreme serpent of the sky, Damballah, and Ayida Wedo, the earth spirit, left Africa with the ancient knowledge of Voodoo. Damballah took the route under the ocean, while Ayida Wedo arched her serpent body across the sky to make a rainbow. They met, intertwining in an embrace of love, and conceived an egg—Haiti. Their spiritual nectar filtered through all men and women as breast milk and semen. Perhaps you read the book by Wade Davis, or saw the movie *The Serpent and the Rainbow*?"

Perini shook his head, still mulling on the breast milk and semen part.

"For the Voodoo religion, Damballah and Ayida Wedo are like the Genesis story in your Bible, the first man and woman created by God." Beauvoir paused, picking up a pen and paper. "Here. Let me draw it for you."

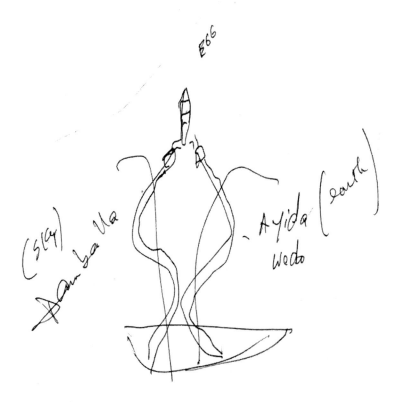

"Are you a practitioner of Voodoo?" Perini asked.

"Yes, indeed, along with 60 million others worldwide. Voodoo is one of the world's oldest known religions. It has been around since the beginning of human civilization—"

Perini held up his hands. "No need to proselytize. I'm not a likely convert. What I'm interested in is finding an old white guy who was pronounced dead at the hospital and was buried in a cemetery, then somehow the man escaped from his coffin and is now wandering around Fort Pierce. Do you know who could make something like that happen?"

Lionel raised his eyebrows. His eyes turned black, almost menacing. "I have no idea."

Perini grimaced, his irritation growing. "Withholding evidence is a serious crime, Beauvoir. You could land in big trouble. I think you know more than you're—"

He heard a faint hiss and a rustling sound behind him. With his heart thumping in his chest, Perini glanced again toward the cage. The python was pressing up against the wire, drawing its head up in an S shape and flicking its tongue directly at the police chief.

"It's Da's feeding time," Beauvoir said, advancing toward the cage. "Want to watch?"

Perini shook his head, said goodbye, and left, thinking, *Everybody lies.*

...7

THE PROFESSOR SMELLED OF OLD SPICE. His arresting black eyes surveyed Bernard Guzman's art collection.

"A pleasure to meet you, Dr. Wolfe," Louissant said in an accented, melodious voice. His handshake was firm, and his smile seemed sincere and genuine, but his eyes bored into Wolfe with an unwelcome intensity. "I had no idea Mr. Guzman's collection was so inclusive; so many works by Haitian First Generation artists: Rigaud Benoit, Castera Bazile, Wilson Bigaud, Jasmin Joseph, Philome Obin, Robert St. Bryce, and I see three paintings by the father of Haitian naive art, Hector Hyppolite."

"Could you explain naive art?" Wolfe asked.

"Artwork produced by self-taught, untrained talents like your own American artist, Grandma Moses. In Haiti, naive art frequently included supernatural visions painted by Voodoo artists who claimed they painted under the influence of their spirits."

Wolfe nodded slowly, amused. "My taste is less hallucinatory. I prefer van Gogh."

Louissant laughed. "Van Gogh and Hyppolite had much in common. Before he became an artist, Van Gogh planned to be a preacher like his father before him. Similarly, Hyppolite was a Voodoo priest, like his father and grandfather. There were instances when van Gogh, like Hyppolite, painted in a possessed state with bursts of high energy. In a letter to his brother Theo in 1888, written from Arles, van Gogh claimed his hands were guided by a force so powerful that his work was produced unconsciously. It was during this period that he famously cut off the lower lobe of his left ear and sent it to a prostitute—"

"I appreciate the fact that your specialty is art, professor," Wolfe interrupted. "Mine is psychiatry. Think of the range of van Gogh's symptoms: hallucinations, depression followed by exaltation and bursts of high energy, followed in their turn by thoughts of despair and

31

spasmodic alcoholism. I would diagnose that the man was painting while suffering from bipolar syndrome, not communing with supernatural spirits."

Louissant's quick smile was abrupt and unsettling. He nodded graciously.

Wolfe continued, "The other night, Guzman told me about an American who opened a school in Port-au-Prince to try and teach art to the natives."

"A racist concept," Louissant said angrily. "It's true that Dewitt Peters was the catalyst who enabled a number of Haitians to paint fulltime and not squeeze in their painting when they weren't driving cabs, preaching, or doing manual labor. But, it is erroneous and insulting to believe that Haitians had to wait for Peters to discover their hidden talents. In my opinion, these First Generation artists knew quite well what they were doing. They did not join the Center to learn to paint, but to get free art supplies and the opportunity to find a wider market and higher prices for their works. Naive art didn't spring from a vacuum. I believe it developed over hundreds of years, in sacred objects and decorations of Voodoo temples."

Wolfe pointed to a painting on masonite. "Not to belabor my point, but this looks like a Haitian Paul Revere painted by a child, not someone under the influence of spirits."

"The crudeness, as you see it, contributes to the expressive power of the image. Hyppolite's two-dimensional paintings are colorful and symbolic. He painted with brushes made of chicken feathers and furniture enamel. The painting you're looking at is Hyppolite's famous *Ogou on His Charger.* Ogou is the Haitian warrior spirit," Louissant explained. "Ogou is depicted wearing a red military uniform, riding a white horse, brandishing a sword or a machete. People who are possessed by Ogou wear a red scarf and adopt the lively language of soldiers seasoned with coarse oaths." Louissant laughed. "They chew cigars and demand rum in the time-honored phrase: '*Grén mwé fret.*' "

"Which means?"

"My testicles are cold."

"Catchy phrase," Wolfe said. "I'll have to remember it when we go north."

Louissant continued, "Hyppolite achieved worldwide recognition in 1947 when his work was featured at the international UNESCO exhibit in Paris."

Preston Dorsett said, "Here's another one by that Hyppolite fellow. Under the circumstances with Mr. Guzman, it's kind of prophetic —zombies."

"It's called *Les Zombis*," Louissant commented.

"As a Haitian, how do you feel about zombies and Voodoo?" Wolfe asked.

Louissant smiled without warmth. "Zombies are a combination of pagan superstition and group hysteria; a pitiless exploitation of the poor by charlatans. There's nothing supernatural about the Voodoo

phenomenon. The only good thing Voodoo produces is a source for artists."

Preston Dorsett pointed to a painting with three ghostlike figures. "Phillipe," he said. "Is this an example of Voodoo art?"

"This painting is called *The Loa*," Louissant said. "Painted by Robert Saint-Bryce, a Voodoo priest who found painting a vehicle for the expression of his religion. His tadpole men and loa trinity have the power of primitive expression comparable to totems or Indian amulets."

"What's a loa?" Dorsett asked

"In Haiti it is common knowledge that the loa are not just distant abstract spirits, but are a central part of Voodoo. They act as intermediaries between human beings and the creator, called Bondye or Good-God, not unlike saints and angels do in Catholicism."

Louissant walked around the room studying the thirty paintings. "Ah. André Pierre," he said, exhaling slowly. "This amazing painting is entitled *The Three Loa*. It's three versions of Erzulie by Andre Pierre, a mystic and one of the great names of Haitian art. On the right you see red-eyed Erzulie Danto, a petro spirit with a stormy disposition. Notice the heart pierced by a sword: that's the mark of Erzulie Danto.

"The center figure is Erzulie Frieda: goddess of love, a light-skinned mulattress. The Erzulie on the left is Maitress Congo, who personifies Africa, the sacred homeland of Haitian ancestors."

Wolfe wandered into Bernard Guzman's den. There was only one painting in the room. Against the white wall, he observed the disturbing scene. Trees in the picture appeared dead. A dozen villagers were confronting with sticks a horrifying beast: a dark figure with wings—clutching a child.

He studied the artist's signature in the lower right. "Phillipe," Wolfe called out. "Wasn't Rigaud Benoit one of the First Generation artists you mentioned? Come in and take a look at his creepy painting."

Louissant stiffened; his eyes turned cold and hardened. Collecting himself, the professor said, "Yes, this work is by Benoit." With a bare smile he added, "In Haitian folklore there are fantasies of flying

witches and werewolves called loup garous. But, you must understand that Haiti is a country with a high illiteracy rate, so ridiculous superstitions are rampant."

Dorsett glanced at his watch. "Dr. Wolfe, one reason I wanted you to meet Professor Louissant was to describe the missing nude painting that you mentioned to Chief Perini."

"I only had a few minutes to wander around," Wolfe reflected. "I thought that Bernie's collection was amazing. The painting I liked most was a dark-skinned nude woman in a dense forest of brilliantly colored birds and flowers."

"Sounds like a typical painting of Erzulie," Louissant responded without enthusiasm. "Erzulie is a commonplace subject for Haitian artists, like the assembly line kitsch tourists buy of thatched roofs and market scenes. Without seeing the actual painting, I couldn't comment."

Wolfe asked, "How much is Guzman's collection worth?"

"A proper evaluation of thirty paintings takes time and research. The condition of each painting and its provenance must be carefully checked."

"Give us a ballpark estimate."

Louissant looked at Dorsett, who nodded an approval.

"The good news is that the Haitian government declared 2009 as the year of Hector Hyppolite. I attended a retrospective exhibition of the work of Hyppolite in Washington, D.C., at the Art Museum of the Americas in May. Therefore his work is in demand."

"And the bad news?"

"With the economy in a slump, the auction houses are not having a good year. Nonetheless, three Hyppolites at high six figures, and twenty-five others averaging at least $50,000 each. That's roughly three plus million."

Dorsett whistled.

"Gentlemen," Wolfe concluded. "If Bernard Guzman's collection is worth over three million at auction, and probably more if sold off individually, isn't it passing strange that someone would steal only one painting and leave a fortune in artwork on the walls?"

...8

EARLY TWENTIES, DORSETT GUESSED, eyeing the attractive young woman sitting across from him in Guzman's living room. He observed her dark almond-shaped eyes and honey-colored skin. Josi Beauvoir was dressed in sandals; tight, faded jeans; and a black, vee-necked T-shirt that directed the man's attention to her cleavage. His eyes unwillingly riveted on the girl's barely contained breasts. Closing his eyes behind dark glasses, he tried to still his thoughts. *Not exactly my idea of a cleaning lady.*

"My name is Dorsett, Miss Beauvoir. I'm consulting with the police in regard to Mr. Bernard Guzman's mysterious disappearance." He displayed his FBI identification.

The young woman stuck her hand out. "Call me Josi."

Dorsett sniffed her perfume, subtle and feminine. "We're checking out everyone who saw Mr. Guzman prior to his accident. When you entered this apartment on the day he collapsed, did you notice anything unusual?"

The young woman returned his smile, then sighed. She rolled her eyes and tossed her head back. "More unusual than seeing a man vomiting, turning blue, and not able to breathe?"

Dorsett knew that the proscribed technique to avoid answering an awkward question was to immediately ask another. "Please tell me exactly what happened when you entered that day."

She shrugged. "I knocked—no one answered. I have keys to all of my customers' units. Mr. Guzman was lying on the carpet gasping for breath. I thought he was choking and considered trying the Heimlich maneuver, but the man looked in really bad shape, so I called 911."

"How long before the ambulance arrived?"

"It seemed forever, but probably no more than ten minutes. Why are you questioning me? Is it because I'm Haitian?"

Dorsett blinked. "Of course not."

"Do you think I cast a Voodoo spell on the man?"

Dorsett stared at her in astonishment. She had a stubborn look in her eye. "Miss Beauvoir, Voodoo spells are a little out of the FBI's purview, and—"

Her eyes blazed. "What is your FBI's purview? You were caught with your pants down on September eleventh when the terrorists were getting flight instruction just up the road in Vero Beach. Now you're conducting electronic surveillance on U.S. citizens. You might as well chase zombies—they can't hire lawyers and sue you."

Dorsett was jolted by Josi's hostility. "Young lady, we've gotten off on the wrong foot," he said in a stern voice. "You needn't be defensive. I would appreciate your cooperation. These are just routine background questions I intend to ask you. Okay?"

Her eyes flickered. "If you promise not to sound so pompous."

"Excuse me?"

"You're on the government's payroll. I'm not. I get paid for cleaning apartments. I don't get paid for chitchat. While I think you're a great-looking older guy, if I'm not under arrest, I have to get back to work." She rose to leave.

"Hold on a minute," Dorsett said, raising his hands in mock surrender. "Let's start over and I will try and be less... pompous."

She sat down and looked at him, openly interested. "Okay. Why did you join the FBI?"

Dorsett brooded. *What the fuck, now she's questioning me?* He took a breath, rethinking the seriousness of his mission, and forced a smile on his face. "It's a long story. As a kid, I was raised in segregated Alabama about the time Governor Wallace blocked the entrance of blacks into the university. I was good at sports, made the high school All-State football team; I ended up with a full scholarship to the same University of Alabama. It was before you were born, but in 1979 Alabama won the national championships, and I was drafted by the Miami Dolphins."

"How exciting," she said in a soft, kittenish voice.

"The Dolphins picked me to back up Larry Little, their top defensive lineman. Little wasn't about to turn his job over to a rookie. I was cut before the opening game with Buffalo."

"I'm sorry," Josi said, brushing lightly against Dorsett's tightly muscled forearm.

"I was disappointed, not playing pro ball, but from early on I wanted to either be a history teacher like my mother, or in the criminal justice system. Being a black kid in the South, I witnessed racism first-hand; it made me feel degraded and angry."

"I can relate."

"I joined the bureau, didn't screw up, and ended up in the FBI field office in Miami."

"You talk about feeling degraded and angry—how about the way the government discriminates against Haitian refugees?"

"What are you talking about?"

"I'm talking plain, unadulterated racism. Ninety-five percent of the Haitian boat people who complete the dangerous water crossing are forcibly returned. But Cuban refugees who reach our shores are allowed to stay and become legal residents. That's discrimination."

"I don't make the laws," Dorsett pointed out. "Cubans can stay because they are escaping from a Communist regime. According to Congress, Haitians are leaving a so-called democracy, so they are forc-ibly returned. FBI agents don't get involved in politics. As a black man," Dorsett stared hard and added, "this double immigration stan-dard does piss me off. You understand what I'm sayin'—girl?"

Josi placed one hand on her hip and cocked her body in his direc-tion. "And is there a Mrs. Dorsett with five little ones at home?"

"No. Maybe I'm a hard man to please."

"They say a hard man is good to find."

Dorsett blushed, but couldn't think of a reply.

"Times are changing, Preston. Haitians have come a long way from being immigrants and boat people. North Miami just elected a Haitian-American mayor and city council. We'll develop political clout too. But I'm still telling you the current U.S. immigration policy sucks."

Dorsett smiled. "Agreed. Now it's your turn." He took out his small notepad.

"I'll make this short. I'm running late. I attended Indian River

State College," Josi began, "and worked part-time for a condo-cleaning company. I wanted to be a computer programmer, but things got financially tight at home so I had to work full-time. Last year I was able to secure a small business loan and purchased a condo cleaning franchise. Now I have my own company."

"Do you live with your family?"

"I've always lived with Tata, my grandmother. My mother died in childbirth; I never knew my father. Tata says that after Mama died, Papa went to work the sugar fields and never came back."

"Where were you born?"

"In a little hill-town in Haiti, Ville-Bonheur."

He continued to make entries in his book. "And your mother's name?"

"Jacqui."

"Your father's?"

"I use Tata's family name, Beauvoir."

"What does your grandmother do?"

"Tata works part-time; mainly she's a *mambo*."

"A what?"

"She's a priestess in the Fort Pierce Voodoo community."

He looked up sharply. "Voodoo?"

"Don't go Hollywood on me, Preston. Americans don't understand Haiti, and what they understand least is Voodoo. Makes them think of crazy niggers in mud, black dolls with pins, and zombies running around attacking people—"

Dorsett interrupted, "Does she use the zombie powders?"

Josi shrugged her shoulders. "Whether zombies are the result of powders, drugs, or people suffering from mental problems, I don't know. Some folks say 'zombie' is a metaphor for the Haitian people. Our ancestors were sold into slavery and like zombies, removed from their families forever. Zombies are put in caskets just like slaves were forced to lie in the belly of slave ships. Slaves were treated a lot like zombies—forced to work as slaves on plantations."

He persisted. "I'm curious about how people become zombies and what chemicals are used to revive them."

"Come to dinner Friday and ask my grandmother." Josi grinned at him. "If you don't accept, I'll tell Tata to put a hex on you and turn you into a loup-garou."

"What's that?"

"A loup-garou is a Haitian werewolf, sweetie, so you better show up. I really have to get back to work." Josi blew a kiss off the palm of her hand.

After she left, Dorsett snapped open his cell phone and punched in a series of numbers. When a voice answered, he whispered, "Dorsett here. Things are moving faster than I expected."

"We're counting on you," the voice said. "Our future is at stake."

...9

"IT'S GOT TO OVER BE A HUNDRED DEGREES," Dominick Perini said to Wolfe, wiping his perspiring forehead with a large handkerchief. "The station is crawling with media. I wouldn't be surprised if Anderson Cooper broadcast from an open grave tonight on CNN."

"Something cold to drink?" Wolfe asked. "Beer, soda, water?"

"On a steamy day like this, a cold brewski is medicinal. Right, doctor?"

"How's the case coming?" Wolfe asked, returning with a cold beer.

Perini took a gulp. "It's been my experience that the first twenty-four hours of an investigation are the most critical. Every day after that, with no new evidence, our chances diminish exponentially. We've checked ingress and egress, and all the good stuff—forensic evidence, ingested stomach contents, witnesses' motives, everything that might form a chain leading to answers." He shook his head. "*Nada.* We're continuing to check out the suspects."

"Me included?"

"One beer is not enough of a bribe to exclude you entirely."

"No jury would ever convict me of going to a damp graveyard late at night, with my arthritis. And then, of course, I dug up the dead body and gave it my wife's chicken soup so that the poor soul could work on my sugar cane plantation in Palm Beach Gardens."

Perini shrugged. "After you, there's the cleaning woman, and Guzman's girlfriend."

"Forget Josi Beauvoir," Wolfe interrupted. "That girl is a gem. A hardworking young woman. Millie and I are having dinner at her grandmother's tomorrow night."

"Everybody lies," Perini said. "In my business, I've seen honest, hardworking people do unexpected things. At the moment, I'm focusing on Honey Crabtree and her husband, Norman. Honey worked for the company that manages your condominium. That's how she met Guzman. Word has it your condo president offered Mrs. Crabtree an offer she couldn't refuse: multiple orgasms and the opportunity of making serious nontaxable income."

Wolfe nodded. "Money and sex are powerful stimuli."

"Guzman was planning to skip. He signed a contract with a local real estate firm. If he was leaving her to face arrest, Honey would have a motive for killing him. And, she had a pass key to his apartment. Her alibi is that on Tuesday night she visited her sick mother in Orlando."

"Doesn't that clear her?"

"The old lady lives alone, has Alzheimer's and doesn't know what time of day it is."

"How about the woman's husband? Jealousy is a strong motivation."

"A cuckolded husband, who is also a professional exterminator, would make any cop's A list. Norman is experienced at killing pests, particularly one who crawled into his wife's pants."

"Is it confirmed that Bernard *was* poisoned?"

"Yes, I got the report in from the Orlando lab." Perini shook his head. "I know Norman Crabtree. It's a stretch to see him as a murderer. We also know Honey wasn't with her mother in Orlando. She was dining with Guzman at Bahama Mama's Restaurant in Jensen Beach."

"How do you know that?"

"Pure luck, not clever detecting. The *Fort Pierce Tribune* ran a piece about the missing condo president. A waiter at the restaurant recognized Guzman's face from the newspaper article. He told his boss, who called us."

Wolfe fetched two more beers.

Perini scanned his note pad. "I thought it worth a try to run his name through the NCIC computer to see if anything lit up. After all the years in this business, I have friends. The National Crime Information Center drew a blank, but it hitchhiked to a watch list from the Food and Drug Administration. According to FDA computer records, Guzman's father's company was suspected of drug adulteration. To avoid prosecution, the old man transferred his operation to Haiti, where labor was cheaper and quality control nonexistent. After that, the government tried to keep close tabs on the Guzman family."

Perini took another drink and flipped a page. "Bernard Guzman married a young Haitian girl. When his wife became pregnant, he wanted no kids and insisted upon an abortion. She refused, so your friend Bernard sent her packing, back to her family in rural Saut d'Eau. With no doctors and no hospital in the area, Mrs. Guzman died in childbirth with a breech baby. Her death was in the paper; the FDA computers had been programmed to pick up Guzman's name."

"On Guzman's behalf," Wolfe said, "he helped a lot of people by supplying the drug that cures onchocerciasis, the river blindness disease."

Perini ignored Wolfe's comment on Guzman's behalf. "Here are the Orlando lab results." He reached into his pocket. "I need my glasses for this small type. Here we are. Subject, Bernard Guzman, was an overweight male of sixty-seven years, five foot seven, a hundred and ninety pounds. Tracings found in the stomach contained two marine species: the poison *fufu–diodon hystrix L*, and the sea toad, or *crapaud du mer–Spheroids testudineus*."

"What's that in plain English?"

"They found tracings of puffer fish, which belongs to a tropical order of fish that carry the poison tetrotoxin in their bodies."

Wolfe nodded. "Tetrotoxin *is* one of the deadliest substances found in nature. Like any drug, its effects depend on dosage and method of administration. So what does it mean, Chief?"

"We don't know when Guzman ingested the substance or its efficacy, so we can't tie it in to a specific suspect or time. The one thing we are now certain of is that Guzman *was* poisoned." Perini scratched his head. "He wasn't killed for money. Guzman's assets are intact. There is six hundred thousand in his bank account, not including what he embezzled from the condo. The apartment must be worth close to eight-fifty, plus his art collection. His net worth total is well over three million dollars, with no known relatives."

The captain's phone beeped. "Chief," the switchboard operator said. "Are you near a TV? Turn it on Channel Five—quick. More zombies."

...10

"WE INTERRUPT OUR CHANNEL FIVE PROGRAM for a special report: This afternoon the Palm Beach Sheriff's Department responded to dozens of cell phone calls from terrified tourists and shop owners along Palm Beach's Worth Avenue. Two female zombies wearing flowered hats were reported loitering in front of a posh French restaurant in the Via Mizner arcade. Eyewitnesses described the two creatures as pale, mute, jaundiced-looking old women with glazed, vacant eyes and shuffling walks. Arriving on the scene, Sheriff Bunkie Trueheart handcuffed and apprehended the zombies, then addressed the swarm of bystanders, news reporters and TV cameras. Here is a rebroadcast of Sheriff Trueheart's remarks."

Television viewers could see a short, thickset man with a roll of fat that pressed hard against his belt. He wore a holstered nine-millimeter pistol on his right hip.

"I ain't no hero," the sheriff said in a high-pitched, wheezing voice. "Great gawdamighty, I just seen my duty and I done it. In Palm Beach, we don't let zombies run around loose, like they do up Fort Pierce way."

The Channel Five announcer added, "The Worth Avenue crowd cheered their sheriff. The alleged zombies have been remanded to the Palm Beach jail, under heavy guard."

AT THE POLICE STATION, a seething Babs Merriweather identified her grandmother. "You idiots," she screamed at the police. "This is my grandmother, Penelope Merriweather, and her sister Minnie. They live at Happy Acres Nursing Home. Both have mild dementia. It's Grandma's ninety-first birthday; I was taking them to lunch at Suzette's Restaurant. I dropped them off in front of the restaurant while I parked the car." She paused to catch her breath. "The next thing I know, fatso here," she said, pointing an angry finger at Sheriff Trueheart, "is carting my family off in handcuffs."

"Now just a gol-dern minute, ma'am," Trueheart said. "How was I to know—"

"Shut up, asshole," Babs barked. "Explain it to my lawyer."

The Merriweather sisters were released from police custody and escorted out the back door of the station house to avoid the horde of reporters and TV crews. Penelope said, "This was the best birthday party ever."

Aunt Minnie was also in high spirits. "Can we do this again next year?"

"I'll sue the bastards," Babs hissed, feeling another spell of morning sickness coming on.

"Who knocked you up, honey?" Aunt Minnie asked.

Arriving home, Babs rechecked the pregnancy test confirming the presence of gonadotropin in her urine, then surfed the Internet searching for a personal injury lawyer. Stumbling upon the web site of Elvar T. Pfarr, she dialed toll-free 1-800-GET EVEN.

ELVAR PFARR FLEW TO PALM BEACH and was retained to represent the Merriweather family in an unlawful arrest suit against the City of Palm Beach. Pfarr, an undersized, precise little man, arranged for a news conference at the Happy Acres Nursing Home. The Happy Acres' owners, learning of the impending arrival of the press, immediately hired a landscaping crew and two English-speaking nurses and had the dingy lobby repainted overnight.

When the news conference began, Pfarr, dressed in a plain dark suit, dark nondescript tie, and ordinary white shirt, proclaimed, "The reputations of these dignified elderly ladies have been sullied and their health damaged by the crude and violent treatment inflicted by the Palm Beach police. Not since 1997 when Abner Louima, a poor, innocent Haitian immigrant, had a mop handle stuck up his rear end while in police custody in New York City, have human beings been so degraded."

The crowd of tottering nursing home residents waved their canes in the air. "Tell 'em, Shorty," they chanted.

Pfarr continued, "Physical and mental abuse is unacceptable in our society today. Only by the City of Palm Beach paying restitution to these poor women, who were insulted, assaulted, handcuffed and arrested, will people realize justice doesn't only apply to abused children and battered wives. It applies to our aged parents too."

Palm Beach County officials, aware of the nine-million-dollar amount that New York City paid Abner Louima, agreed to a large, undisclosed settlement for the Merriweather family. With the consent of all parties, settlement terms remained sealed.

"CONGRATULATIONS, MR. PFARR. My name is Sloan," said the attractive blonde newspaper reporter. "The *Palm Beach Post* assigned me to interview you."

Pfarr smiled and said nothing.

"Rumor has it that the settlement topped ten million."

"Miss Sloan," said Pfarr. "As you know, the settlement terms are sealed."

"Well then, can you tell me about yourself, sir?"

"Certainly. I graduated law school at U of G."

"University of Georgia?"

"No. University of Grenada. After graduation, I accepted a job in New York City with the federal government as an interstate commerce lawyer. When the Clinton administration came into office, they replaced me, under the Fair Employment Act of 1992, by a black lesbian law-school dropout whose mother was one-fifth Native American."

The reporter snorted with laughter. "That's a scream. You could be a standup comic."

"Well, it wasn't funny to me," Pfarr bristled. "On the day I was fired, I was seriously despondent, contemplating suicide. As I walked aimlessly down a street in New York, I observed police on horseback manhandling a crowd of indigent homeless people outside of a discount mattress store. The company, Bob's Waterbeds, was running a promotion for people to come in and test their mattresses. The mob shoved me into a Kinko's store, where I had the presence of mind to have business cards and client forms printed while I waited."

Sloan was howling with delight. "Of course you did. Then what happened?"

Elvar grinned proudly. "I returned to the melee and signed up fifty clients for a class-action personal injury suit. Broadway Bob settled out of court, and I was in business."

The *Palm Beach Post* reporter wiped her eyes. "I can understand why you're successful," she said, still giggling. "With your great sense of humor, juries must love you." The reporter winked. "And I'm sure you know about the alleged zombie in Fort Pierce?"

"Huh?" Pfarr responded. "Where's Fort Pierce?"

...11

TATA BEAUVOIR'S HOUSE sat on a tired-looking street off of Avenue D in Fort Pierce. The two-story, brown clapboard residence had paint-cracked white shutters and a lawn overgrown with weeds.

Millie Wolfe waited while Max pressed the doorbell. It didn't work, so he knocked. The door was opened by a woman in her late seventies, stooped yet stoic-looking, with a massive, round black face. Her eyes were heavy-lidded but piercing behind large, unfashionable eyeglasses.

"*Bonjour*—you come in, sit down. I Josi's grandma, Tata." The old woman plodded heavily back into the living room. "Josi home soon. You like kleren?" Not waiting for a reply, she filled two jelly jars.

"What's kleren?" Wolfe asked, curious.

"You try it, mon. See it work for you."

He sipped the sweet-smelling raw rum and coughed. Beads of sweat gathered on Wolfe's forehead. His eyes teared. "Good stuff," he croaked.

Josi rushed in, kissed her grandmother, offered apologies and ran upstairs. To fill the awkward silence, Wolfe said, "Josi says you're a priestess."

"Friends, they got trouble—you know: work, love, sickness—they come to me. People give me money: two dollars, ten dollars, whatever, because they grateful. I love to make treatment. It be a strain sometime, people come all hours, day and night. 'Tata, I got this. Tata, I got that, you got to help me.' I just go and do it. When I heal people, and they happy, make me feel good."

"Is healing something passed down in your family?" Millie inquired.

"That's the truth." Tata grinned with white teeth. "My momma show me how to do good. In Haiti, they *kouche* me—make me mam-

53

bo. When I come to Fort Pierce people visit me, people who lose job, people who sick, people who got husband or wife problem—I fix them. I say, what you think, you can leave everything to God? You think God got nothing to do but watch out for you? God got problems herself. She too busy. You got to help yourself."

Josi rejoined them. Millie said, "You have a lovely granddaughter."

"Josi gotta get a man."

"Come on, Tata, let's not get into that again."

"Nobody don't get younger. Right? You need somebody. Let me tell you girl, life is struggle. You leave your mamma's belly, you got to fight for what you need—"

Tata was interrupted by the entrance of a slim, narrow-faced man with a clipped, gray drooping mustache. Preston Dorsett trailed in behind him.

"Meet my friend Preston and Uncle Lionel," Josi said, introducing Tata's fifty-year-old son. "Lionel is a *houngan*, a Voodoo priest."

"How exciting!" Millie said. "Like a witch doctor—"

Wolfe interrupted. "Have you heard the one about the Jewish girl bringing her black fiancé home to meet the parents? As they walk into the house the young man is dressed in a loin cloth with a bone embedded in his hair and a big gold ring stuck in his nose. The mother takes one looks and says, 'Bernice, I said marry a rich doctor, not a witch doctor.' "

"Go easy on the kleren, Max," Millie chided him.

"I hadn't heard that one, Dr. Wolfe," Lionel responded. "But I did hear there's a big controversy on the Jewish view of when life begins. In Jewish tradition, the fetus is not considered viable until after it graduates from medical school."

"Touché." Wolfe laughed.

"In Haiti we don't have witch doctors," Lionel explained. "As a *houngan*, I serve the spirits, but I also have a full-time job teaching at Indian River State College."

"What does a houngan do?" asked Dorsett, sipping the kleren.

"In Haiti, with so few doctors, the houngan has to be a doctor, a psychotherapist, and a social worker. Through him, the cosmic forces are manifested."

"Cosmic forces?" Wolfe groaned.

Lionel smiled and shrugged. "People scoff at what they don't understand. In Voodoo, spiritual cosmic forces are called *loa*, from the Fon word *lo*, meaning mystery. The loa are supernatural beings that enter the bodies of mortals through possession during Voodoo ceremonies, giving pronouncements and predictions."

"Tell them about Da, Uncle Lionel."

He laughed. "I have a pet python named Da, after Damballah, the supreme snake spirit and symbol of the ancient African kingdom of Dahomey."

"You really keep a python in the house?" Wolfe asked.

"Yes, and I never lock my doors. But I didn't come tonight to proselytize about Voodoo or tell snake stories, I came to taste Mama's Haitian cooking."

"Are you familiar with zombie powders?" Dorsett asked.

Lionel and his mother exchanged glances. "*Bourik chajé pa kampé*," Tata said, ignoring Dorsett's question. "The table is served, let's eat."

"Tata's cooked a traditional meal," Josi announced. "*Duriz ac pois colle*: stewed chicken, brown rice with black peas, boiled green plantains, and white yams."

"Do I smell lime?" Millie said.

Lionel nodded. "In Haitian food, everything is rubbed, washed or marinated with lime. It doesn't matter what: plantains, chicken, pork —lime is one of the things giving it the tangy flavor. For example, when Tata bakes her chicken, the bottom of the cast iron pan is first lined with plantains, sliced lengthwise, and then doused with lots of lime juice."

Josi piped in, "Next comes the chicken, which Tata marinates in a mixture of orange and the lime juice. To that, she adds plenty of yellow hot peppers, thyme, rosemary and a mixture of red and white beans and bakes it in the oven."

"Delicious!" said Millie, turning to Tata. "I must try your recipe. How much lime juice and how many peppers and plantains?"

The old woman shrugged her shoulders and said, "*Lagniappe.*"

Millie looked at Lionel, who explained, "*Lagniappe* is a Cajun word meaning 'a little this and a little that.' "

Between bites, Wolfe said, "Preston introduced me to a university professor who said Voodoo was staged theater."

The air crackled with tension. Millie kicked him under the table.

"Every religion has its charlatans," Lionel answered. "You've seen TV showmen parading as religious evangelists asking gullible Americans to send in money. Real Voodoo isn't staged theater. Adherents ask what people have always asked of religion: a remedy for their ills, satisfaction of their needs, and hope of survival."

"Can people believe in Voodoo and still be Catholics?" Dorsett asked.

"The Catholic Church has a problem with that, but we don't. We all have a lot to learn from one another. Both religions believe in a supreme being. Our Voodoo loa resemble Christian saints in that they were once people who led exceptional lives. The loa communicate the same message as the old saints and patriarchs—that divinity is here for us now with proper service and contemplation."

"It's over my head." Wolfe yawned.

Lionel exhaled. "I hope you can appreciate that Voodoo is not black magic or devil worshiping. Possession is not psychotic episodes, mass hypnosis, nor staged theater like your professor friend implied. Voodoo is a complex religious system. When possession takes place, the person's body temporarily belongs to the loa who inhabits it, or 'mounts it.' It is the loa who speak through the individual possessed. Sometimes female gods, like Erzulie, possess men who dress up in women's clothing."

"Men dress up in women's clothing?" Preston echoed, as Josi refilled his kleren glass.

"Didn't your FBI have a boss like that?" she said.

Dorsett ignored her remark. He leaned closer to Lionel, whispering, "You houngans know about zombie powders, don't you?"

Lionel patted him on the shoulder. "This is not the moment for such talk."

Tata handed a small paper bag to Millie and whispered in her ear. Both women giggled.

Wolfe was lightheaded from the kleren. "I saw a scary painting in Bernard Guzman's apartment," he mumbled. "It looked like a flying werewolf. The hotshot professor said it was a myth of Haitian folklore—a loup garou."

Hearing the words *loup garou*, Tata scowled and put her finger to her lips. "*Tout moun konnin sa: lé mal égzist.* Everyone knows the evil one exists."

"I LIKE YOUR FAMILY," Dorsett told Josi as she walked him to his car. "This is awkward for me to say, but when the zombie business is over, I would like to know you better."

" 'Know' as in the biblical sense?"

"Be serious, Josi. I'm older than you, and as my daddy always told me, 'Don't sail out further than you can row back.' "

Josi took Dorsett's solemn face in both hands, gently kissing him on the lips, letting her tongue slip slowly into his unprotesting mouth.

"And as my Tata always told me," she whispered, "*Pa pran chans; pa pédu chans.* If you don't take a chance, you'll never know what you missed."

"YOU ATE LIKE A PIG AND YOU'RE DRUNK," Millie berated her husband on the ride home. "I hope the police don't stop us." She was silent for another minute or two. "Your cholesterol is over two eighty, your blood pressure is high, you need to lose weight, and—"

Wolfe interrupted, licking his lips. "Damn, but that old woman can cook."

"Listen to me, Max," she said. "I don't know why, but I do want to keep you around for while. Myles and Beverly each lost eight pounds in one week at a place called the Paradise Spa in Palm Beach. I think we should go there."

Wolfe patted Millie's knee. "*Farin bon ki ra,*" he said.

"What's that supposed to mean?"

"Lionel told me that's Creole for 'a good wife is rare and precious.' "

"Why, thank you, dear." A small smile played on her lips. "And Tata gave me something for you—an herb that's good for your *zozo.*"

"What's my zozo?"

"That's Creole for your little pecker, darling. It's a Voodoo potion that works like Viagra or Cialis—only ten times better."

"Are you serious?"

Millie gave a theatrical sigh. "You get to try it, mon—if we go to the Paradise Spa."

PART II

THE LOUP GAROU

Tout moun konnin sa: lé mal lougarou égzist.

Everyone knows the evil one exists.

...12

"LISTEN TO THIS DRIVEL," Wolfe said, reading from the spa brochure as Millie drove south on I-95. " 'Reflexology is the practice of applying pressure to parts of the feet, with the goal of encouraging a beneficial effect on other parts of the body.' " Wolfe added, "They use foot baths with hot Dead Sea salts, followed by massaging calves and feet with special mud packs made from low-fat llama milk and mustard plasters. It's crap."

"I'm sure they know what they are doing," Millie said. "Bev raved about the wonderful body massages, facial mud packs, and—"

"Myles said Bev looked great until the mud fell off."

"Very funny. Please don't develop an attitude, and don't talk to people with your officious, psychoanalytic voice. It's not becoming."

An aroma of fresh roses and lavender rushed at them as they drove up to the covered portico of the spa. Coconut palms, festive crimson bougainvillea, creamy white hibiscus with red centers, and dark violet leaves lined the circular driveway.

Wolfe eyed a striking blonde wearing skin-hugging white slacks and an orange halter top, a half-size too tight. "Hi guys," the girl in the too-tight pants said. "Welcome to Paradise Spa. I'm Janine, the reflexologist. Are you vegans?"

Wolfe's eyes remained riveted to her cleavage. "Are we what?"

"Vegans. This is a vegetarian spa; we eat only vegetables."

"If vegetarians eat only vegetables, what do humanitarians eat?"

"Be nice, Max," Millie cautioned. "It's only for a week."

WHILE MILLIE UNPACKED, Wolfe scanned the schedule of spa activities posted on the back of the door. He chuckled and said, "These rules were concocted by a seriously disturbed malpractice lawyer."

Paradise Spa
Rules and Schedule

7:00: **Scenic Walk** (meet in the lobby). Van leaves promptly at 7 a.m. to take you to a safe walking area. Otherwise, walk at your own risk.

8:00: **Breakfast**

9:00: **The Cardio Conditioner** (meet in the aerobics room). Bring a note from your physician authorizing participation. The Paradise Spa bears no responsibility for anyone who dies—no refunds or credits.

10:00: **Aqua Fit** (meet at the pool). No bikinis or thongs for women, or cute little jockstrap swim thingies for male guests.

11:00: **Kickboxing** (meet in the aerobics room). Women only. This aerobic program is too strenuous for men.

12:00: **Lunch**

2:00: **Personal Body Sculpting on the Beach** (meet in lobby). Bring your shades, sunscreen and water. Participants take turns molding each other with sand. Men who think this program is just a good opportunity to feel up women's breasts and pubic areas need not attend.

3:00: **Latin Dancing with Ms. Chicita Juarez** (meet in exercise room). Ms. Juarez is no longer permitted to visit gentlemen in their rooms for private Latin dance lessons or whatever.

6:00: **Dinner**

7:30: **Evening program** (meet in lecture room).

* * *

"HOWDY, WE'RE THE BUNTINGS," a woman said to the Wolfes as they entered the dining area. "I'm Toots, and this here's my daughter, Inez. We call her Sis. Join us."

Toots Bunting was a full-figured woman, stocky, with a round, pleasant face a little wrinkled at the eyes. Her straight corn-colored hair was laced with gray. "I'm here to lose weight, and Sis is keeping me company. She's into turtles."

"Turtles. How interesting," Millie said.

Sis nodded, embarrassed by her mother's effusiveness. "Turtles have been on our planet for millions of years," she said. "Loggerheads are air-breathing reptiles who nest only on tropical beaches where it's warm enough to incubate their eggs."

"Why are they called loggerheads?" Wolfe asked, observing the slightly built woman with close-cropped brown hair, thick spectacles and no make-up.

"The name refers to the turtle's large head, which can grow to ten inches wide. Do you know that fifty thousand loggerhead nests are recorded in Florida annually?"

Max shrugged. "Never thought much about it."

"We go out at night when the female loggerheads crawl up on the beach and lay their eggs. If you're interested, you're welcome to join us."

"Sure, why not?" Wolfe said.

"We meet on the beach in front of the spa at midnight. No flash-lights, please. They disorient the turtles."

The first course was brought by an elderly Latino waitress. "Jewww want soup?"

Wolfe whispered to Millie, "How does she know we're Jewish?"

"She's Cuban," Millie hissed a sigh, "and she's asking if *you* want soup."

"This is vegetarian curried cauliflower soup," Sis said.

Wolfe sipped the ecru-colored broth, made a wry face and shoved the bowl away with the palms of both hands.

"If you don't like it, don't eat it," Millie snapped in a whisper. "Don't embarrass me."

The Latino waitress placed a salad in front of Wolfe.

"Ummm... goodie... weeds," he mumbled, pointing a finger into his open mouth.

"They're flowers," Sis explained. "Vegans make salads made with flowers that are tasty and visibly appealing, like dandelion, sorrel, arugula, red clover, nasturtium and tiger lilies."

"Thanks," Wolfe said. "But I prefer not to eat roadside plants as long as my Social Security check keeps coming in regularly."

The floral salad was followed by the main course.

"What's that, honey?" Toots Bunting asked her daughter.

"Tofu pot pie."

Wolfe stared at the dish in front of him. "What's tofu?"

"Tofu is a favorite in the Far East, made from soy milk. It's a protein source and offers protection to women against breast cancer and to men against prostate cancer."

Wolfe sampled the tofu. "It tastes squishy."

"Have you ever been to the spa before, Toots?" Millie inquired.

"I came last May; drank plenty of water, did the yoga exercises, and walked every morning. And in just fourteen days, I lost two weeks."

The Wolfes smiled politely.

"Are you two going to the evening program?" Sis inquired. "Dr. Basil is speaking on herbal healing."

Wolfe poked at his tofu and whispered to Toots, "How far's the nearest deli?"

"GOOD EVENING, LADIES AND GENTLEMEN, my name is Dr. Charles Basil. I am a physician practicing in Haiti, a *dokte feuilles,* which is Creole for 'leaf doctor.' For twenty years I've worked for the Hospital Albert Schweitzer, which provides patient care for thousands of impoverished people of the Artibonite Valley in Haiti. While I'm a general practitioner by training, I specialize in ethnobotany."

"What's that?" someone asked.

"Ethnobotany is somewhere between anthropology and biology. We find new medicines from plants."

Dr. Basil was tall and slender, with a hawk nose and thick glasses. He wore dust-colored khaki pants and a faded green polo sport shirt. His thinning gray hair was worn in a ponytail.

Basil had the nervous habit of clearing his throat before he spoke. "Our hospital was founded forty-five years ago by Larry and Gwen Mellon. Larry came from a rich family, the Mellons. He went to medical school, then opened a hospital in the poorest country he could find —Haiti. Since Larry's death, the hospital relies on outside help for much of its annual budget, which is why I spend six months fundraising and lecturing in the Palm Beach area."

Basil looked out over his audience and smiled. "Voltaire said: 'Doctors are people who prescribe medicines of which we know little, to cure diseases of which we know less, in human beings of whom we know nothing.'"

The audience laughed.

"For every prescription I write for a pharmaceutical drug, I give out forty for botanicals. I have practiced this way for the last five years, and in that time I have not had a single adverse reaction to any of my remedies. I didn't learn what I know from books; I learned from people who actually treat with plants—Haitian *houngans*."

A hand was raised. "What's a houngan?"

"A male priest or healer. Females are called *mambos*. Throughout Haiti, folk medicine is one of the primary sources of medical care. Haitians say, *'Tout maladi pa maladi dokte.'* Not every sickness can be healed by a medical doctor. There are other ways to be healed as well."

Wolfe nodded silently. "Amen."

"The Haitian population could not have survived without a knowledge of herbalism. It's true, this knowledge may have been arrived at by trial and error, and it is also true that the form in which drugs are administered is crude, often brewed from leaves or roots. The houngan or mambo knows which leaves to brew for indigestion, which for a headache and which for a cold. If a Haitian wakes up without a voice, he is given a strong parsley root to chew on and is rapidly restored. If someone is suffering from shock, he's given coarse salt in a jigger of rum to drink. If someone is bleeding badly, they apply a spider's web to the wound and the blood coagulates immediately, and—"

"As an ethnobotanist," Wolfe interrupted, "have you found any organic substances that can produce zombies?"

"A fascinating subject," Basil replied, not missing a beat. "When I first went to Haiti, my notion of zombies came from horror movies: a corpse in tattered rags, rising from the cemetery in a trancelike state, subservient to some unknown master. This macabre figure has become a part of our Western culture. A person who experiences listlessness may say he feels like a zombie. Do zombies really exist? Some consigned them to fable. Others, including foreign and Haitian physicians, claim some of the accounts are true."

The audience shifted in their seats, listening more attentively.

"At my hospital in the Artibonite Valley, I asked if anyone had ever seen a zombie face to face, or as the Haitians say, '*bab pou bab.*' Nobody had. As I investigated, it became clear that anthropologists on the whole had dismissed zombieism as mumbo-jumbo superstition. Reported cases were ignored. For a phenomenon that so electrified the world, and was used in an explicit, racist way to denigrate both a people and their religion, there was a marked absence of serious academic research."

"Is zombie a Creole word?" someone asked.

"The African origin of the word is 'nzambi,' which means 'spirit of a dead person.' My time is up, but if you're interested in zombieism, it's a fascinating subject and I would be happy to stay longer."

There were murmurs of encouragement from the audience.

"In my experience over the years with Haitian patients, there is no doubt the fear of zombies, or the living dead, is deep and pervasive. During my first year at the hospital, the extraordinary case of Clairvius Narcisse, a supposed zombie, came to national attention in Haiti. Narcisse came to our emergency entrance complaining of fever, body aches, general malaise. He began to spit blood. His condition deteriorated, and at 1:15 p.m., Clairvius Narcisse was pronounced dead." Basil cleared his throat. "I was the attending physician."

The spa audience was riveted.

"One of his sisters, Marie Claire, arrived and identified the body, affixing her thumbprint to the death certificate. The body was placed in cold storage, then taken for burial. Narcisse was buried in a small cemetery north of his village of L'Estere. Later a heavy concrete memorial slab was placed over the grave by the family.

"Eighteen years later, a man walked into the L'Estere marketplace and approached a woman named Angelina Narcisse. He introduced himself by a boyhood nickname, a name that only intimate family members would know. He stated to this woman, a sister, that he had been made a zombie years before by his brother because of a land dispute. He remembered everything that happened afterwards, but was unable to stop it.

"Clairvius Narcisse said he remembered being buried and a nail being driven too hard through the lid of the coffin. The nail gouged his cheek, and he bore the scar to prove it. Hours later, lying in his grave, he heard pounding drums, chanting, and his own name called out three times. Rising from the coffin, he was beaten with sisal ropes and covered in black cloths. Clairvius said he was forced to march to the north of the country until they reached a sugar plantation, where he was put to hard labor. He managed to escape and for years roamed the countryside, only returning when he learned of his brother's death."

Wolfe asked, "Is this a true story, doctor, or part of the evening's entertainment?"

Basil laughed. "I know my story sounds eerie. I can assure you it's true. The Narcisse case generated considerable publicity and even drew the attention of the BBC, which filmed a documentary based on his story. I supplied a copy of the death certificate to Scotland Yard, where forensic experts verified the fingerprints of his sister, Marie Claire. Based on testimony of villagers, family members, and physicians, it was concluded that Narcisse was mistakenly diagnosed as dead, buried alive, and taken from the grave. When Narcisse returned to our hospital for examination, I was again part of the medical team examining him. His psychiatric history was studied by Haiti's leading psychiatrist, who, together with two respected North American colleagues, concluded the case was legitimate."

"And what do you believe, Dr. Basil?" someone asked.

"What do I think?" Basil paused before answering. "First, Narcisse would have had to survive at least six to twelve hours in a sealed coffin beneath the ground. Second, the state of apparent death induced by the drug would have to be so profound as to fool a trained professional. As it turns out, I don't have to delve too far into medical literature to discover that under the proper circumstances, both these conditions can be met."

"No offense, doc," someone said with mild sarcasm. "It sounds ridiculous that a trained doctor can't tell if someone's dead or not."

"Breathing can be checked by a feather or mirror placed beneath the nostrils, but both methods have been found unreliable. The absence of respiration may represent suspension. For example, in India, yogis can reduce their oxygen consumption to levels that would prove lethal to ordinary individuals.

"Under normal conditions a person is dead if his heart ceases to beat for five minutes. A proper medical examination requires equipment that didn't exist in rural Haiti at that time. The importance of the Narcisse case was its proof of the zombie phenomenon; a folk toxin potent enough to bring on a deathlike stupor. Since both the toxin and antidote were organic, their source had to be a plant or animal found in Haiti."

Wolfe raised his hand again. "Dr. Basil, have you ever heard of the puffer fish as a source of the zombie poison?"

"Good point. There is documentary evidence available which attributes that temporary paralysis can occur when one has absorbed the poison from the liver and intestines of the puffer. These species belong to an order of fish called the Tetraodontiformes, which have tetrodotoxin in their bodies. Tetrodotoxin is one hundred thousand times more effective than cocaine, and get this—" The room was hushed. "The toxin induces a state of paralysis, marked by low metabolic levels while the victim remains conscious. The folk poison containing known toxins is capable of inducing a state of apparent death. The symptoms I observed with Clairvius Narcisse matched the symptoms of tetrodotoxin poisoning."

"Are these views shared by the medical community?"

"Additional evidence for zombies comes from Japan, where the flesh of the puffer fish, *fugu*, is considered a delicacy. It is prepared by chefs specially trained and certified by the government to prepare the flesh free of the toxic liver, gonads and skin. Despite these precautions, many cases of tetrodotoxin poisoning are reported each year in patients ingesting *fugu*. Poisonings usually occur after eating fish prepared by uncertified handlers. The end result, in many cases, is death. One woman who appeared to be dead was taken to the morgue in Tokyo. She woke up later and went home."

"I'm a doctor, and I understand what you're saying about the puffer fish and tetrodotoxins," Wolfe said. "But, the question I have is: how is it possible to resurrect a person who has been certified as dead —and buried?"

Basil nodded. "It may be hearsay, or nonsense, or true, but I've been told that when a zombie is taken from the grave, it is force-fed a paste. The ingredients of the paste are sweet potato, cane sugar, and a plant called *datura*, also known as the 'Holy Flower of the North Star.' It's getting late. Shall I continue?" Basil asked

By way of answer, he was greeted by unanimous applause.

"Datura can create a state of psychotic delirium, marked by confusion and amnesia. Administered to someone suffering the effects of tetrodotoxin poisoning, and who has been buried alive, the devastating physical and psychological results are difficult to imagine. That explains why resurrected zombies look like the walking dead. It's late, but I'll take one final question."

Toots Bunting raised her hand. "Are you married or single?"

"Mo-therrrr," groaned Sis Bunting.

...13

"SPA LADIES, YOUR ATTENTION PLEASE," the beach walk leader said. "On this historic spot, our beautiful state of Florida was founded and christened. Yes, right here. On the fourteenth of October, 1520. Ponce de Leon and his men ran amok, raping and sodomizing the beautiful local Calusa Indian women, who wore flowers in their hair. This memorable event prompted Ponce de Leon to give the conquered territory its future statehood name: 'Feast of Flowers, or *Pasqua de Florida.*'"

"That's disgusting," Millie said.

"Lately there has been a rash of assaults and muggings in this hallowed area. Therefore, the spa advises all participants in the 'safe scenic beach walk' not to stray far from the group. We don't want a repeat of the 'Feast of Flowers,' do we, ladies?"

While Millie participated in the "safe scenic beach walk," Wolfe swam in the spa pool. After two laps, he experienced painful leg cramps, climbed out and took a few deep breaths to calm himself.

A tanned, wrinkled, elderly woman looked up from her reading. "How was your swim?"

He shifted uncomfortably, massaging his sore calves. "Short but invigorating."

"I'm Rachel Walters."

Wolfe nodded slightly. "Nice to meet you, Rachel. I'm Max."

"I wanted to do the beach walk," she said. "But I'm too exhausted from traveling here."

He continued to rub his leg muscles. "Where were you traveling from?"

"I was rafting down the Colorado River."

Wolfe studied the woman's eyes. She was serious. "And when you're not rafting, do you bungee jump and wind surf?"

Removing her reading glasses, Rachel said, "I'm eighty-seven years old. Rafting the Colorado was something I've always wanted to do before I died—that, and to travel to the Mesa Verde in Southeast Colorado and see the Anasazi tribal grounds. Anasazi is Navajo for 'ancient ones,' you know. They lived in stone dwellings as far back as 750 A.D. They were the ancestors to the Hopi and other Pueblo Native Americans."

"What are you reading?"

"Tony Hillerman's book *Skinwalkers.*"

"Skinwalkers?"

"They're evil demons, like werewolves. In Mesa Verde I met an old Navajo woman, about my age. She told me about witches who stalk the night wearing animal skins or owl feathers. The Navajo name they use to describe the witches is *yena Losi.*"

Wolfe laughed. "As a psychologist, I've never been a believer in supernatural beings."

Rachel swept a strand of white hair out of her eyes. "That's not surprising, but how then do you account for the pandemic of vampires and werewolves in movies and on TV?"

He shrugged. "This current obsession with werewolves and vampires may originate from deep repressed memories of when our ancestors were primates and hunters. Before we became agricultural gatherers, we were—out of necessity—cannibalistic."

She rolled her eyes. "I may be old, but I'm not gullible."

He raised both hands in a peace gesture. "Part of the popularity of monster films is pure escapism, not unexpected in bad economic times."

Rachel nodded.

Wolfe continued, "And part of the appeal is experiencing the fear sensation in a safe environment, like a movie theater. Vampires and werewolves provide a fantasy of excitement in our mundane 'reality show' lives; powerful figures experiencing wild sexual nocturnal escapades."

She cracked a wry smile. "The old woman I met wasn't seeking wild sex, escapism or immortality, or smoking the divine cactus, peyote. She told me flat out about seeing a yena Losi bothering her sheep. When she went into the hogan to get her rifle to shoot the witch, it saw her coming, turned into a big owl and flew away. And, she also told me about how Navaho witches choose their skins. The coyote skin is for speed. The bear skin is for strength. The owl skin is for flying long distances."

"Rachel," Wolfe said, "you're one interesting lady."

"It's important for people my age to keep active. I own a gallery in Vero Beach. Where are you from, Max?"

"South Hutchinson Island."

"Do you know the art collector, Bernard Guzman?"

"He is—or was—my neighbor."

"I visited Hutchinson Island last month at Mr. Guzman's invitation. He was interviewing art dealers to handle the sale of his collection. Bernard could be abrasive, but he always treated me with respect."

"What's your impression of the collection?"

"The Voodoo paintings captured my attention with their bright colors and stark mysticism," she said. "I love self-taught artists. Their visual energy excites an old woman like me. Over the years, I've seen Haitian art progress from the walls of the Voodoo temples to the walls of top galleries around the world. And of course, Bernard owns originals by Haiti's most important artist, Hector Hyppolite. The timing is ideal to market Hector's paintings, because this year in Haiti is being promoted as 'The Year of Hyppolite.' "

"Yes. I heard that information. Did Bernard hire you?"

She nodded. "It was between us or Vincent Valdesi in Palm Beach. Vincent lives in Haiti half of the year. I think that's why Bernard chose us; we're here full time. We concluded a verbal contract. Life isn't simple, is it?"

"How did you learn about his disappearance?"

"My daughter, Laurie, saw it on CNN. Bernard wanted me to pick up one of his paintings and reframe it before we offered the collection for sale. It was Hector Hyppolite's *Maitress Erzulie*; really breathtaking. When I saw the Erzulie painting, it reminded me of something that a friend of mine, Phoebe Stanton, wrote—"

Rachel was interrupted by Jenine, the curvaceous reflexologist. Wolfe gaped at her tight white short-shorts, red platform shoes and colorful Paradise Spa T-shirt, worn, as usual, a half-size too tight over jiggling breasts. "Hi guys," Jenine said, twisting her blonde ponytail.

"Max," said Rachel. "Meet our spa reflexologist, Jenine."

"You should try reflexology," Jenine cooed.

"I have arthritis. While I was swimming I got a cramp in my calf muscle."

"Let me take a look," the reflexologist said, radiating raw sexual energy. Jenine sat next to Wolfe on the chaise, kneading two fingers against his left calf. "I can enervate nerve endings in your feet and legs, corresponding to every organ in your body. It's better than a massage. How does this feel?"

Her touch came as a physical jolt. Every muscle in Wolfe's foot let go. A warm tingling sensation spread through his groin. His excitement was evident under the towel across his lap.

"These were just a few of your stimulated nerve endings." The reflexologist squeezed his instep and giggled. "Would you like a private session?"

"Let me get back to you on that," Wolfe stammered. Cold sweat trickled down his spine.

After the reflexologist left, Rachel said, "Jenine's got a very superior set of knockers, Max. Take a cold shower, you'll feel better."

RACHEL WALTERS JOINED THE WOLFES at the spa's buffet breakfast. Max sipped the ersatz coffee and turned his eyes heavenward. "I hate it here," he said in a muffled voice.

"The coffee is made from carob," Rachel said. Turning to Millie, she asked, "How was the scenic spa walk?"

"No one was sexually attacked; that disappointed some of the ladies." Millie went on without missing a beat. "Max tells me that you own an art gallery."

"It keeps me young. During World War II, I worked for the U.S. government in Haiti. I was fortunate to be there at the birth of modern Haitian painting. An American watercolorist, Dewitt Peters, came to Haiti and started Le Centre d'Art in Port-au-Prince. Dewitt and I were good friends. We corresponded for years after I returned to the States. I was with Dewitt the day he met the artist Hector Hyppolite."

"Tell us," Millie said, "what happened?"

"One day Dewitt was driving through a village called Mounters. He saw a small bar with doors decorated with tropical birds painted in brilliant colors, set among brightly-colored flowers. Thanks to the Haitian novelist Phillipe Marcel, Dewitt was able to find out who the artist was. The man was a Voodoo priest named Hector Hyppolite. Hector painted the doors using chicken feathers for brushes."

"Fascinating," Millie exclaimed. "Did you ever meet the artist?"

"Oh yes. Dewitt located the hut Hyppolite lived in with his mistress and two little girls. I'll never forget it. He was tall and extremely thin, dressed in striped pajamas. His jet black, wiry hair was parted in the middle and shaved around his ears. The face seemed more Arawak Indian than African. Hector said our visit was no surprise; Maitress Erzulie told him in a dream that a *blanc* would find him, that his life would change, and the world would recognize his artistry."

"That's quite a story," Wolfe said, picking tofu bacon bits out of his imitation egg salad.

Rachel continued, "Dewitt Peters described Hyppolite's pictures as crude, with bulging eyes and grotesque bodies, but he was astounded by Hector's inventiveness, painting mostly on cardboard, with old brushes, chicken feathers, and his fingers to achieve the desired texture."

"Was Hyppolite known outside of Haiti?" Millie asked.

"Dewitt sent his paintings to the UNESCO exhibition in Paris in 1947. They created a sensation. The French critic, Andre Briton, the one who started the Surrealist movement, went so far as to say that Hyppolite could have single-handedly changed the course of contemporary French painting. Then the Museum of Modern Art in New York bought Wilson Bigaud's *Murder in the Jungle*. After that, Haitian painters were no longer looked upon as clumsy innocents."

"Does Haitian art sell well in Vero Beach?"

"Snowbird traffic is from January to Easter, then the summer months are slow. Most people are timid about Haitian art. They're more comfortable with paintings of seagulls and beach scenes to match their pink, green and white decor," she said with a shrug. "But enough about me." She smiled. "How long have you been married?"

"Over fifty years," Wolfe responded. "People ask for the secret of our relationship. We take time out to go to a restaurant two times a week. A little candlelight, dinner, soft music and dancing. Millie goes Tuesdays, I go Fridays."

Rachel's eyes crinkled with amusement. "I know a Henny Youngman joke when I hear one. Concerning our conversation about witch-werewolves, I bought a painting in Arizona that I would like you to see. Can I borrow your husband for a little while this evening, Millie?"

"Only if you promise not to return him."

'THE SPA DIET FOCUSES ON WATER," Rachel said, winking and refilling Wolfe's glass, "but the Rachel Walters diet focuses on Tangueray gin."

"I'm like W.C. Fields," Max responded. "I never drink anything stronger than gin before breakfast." He eyed the painting she had unwrapped. "This is very creepy, Rachel," Wolfe said, putting aside his glass. "What is she?"

"I showed the painting to my Navaho friend. She said it is a painting of a *yena Losi,* which translates into 'He who trots along here and there on all fours.' A yena Losi can transform into a wolf, but different animal skins are used for other transformations. She said that 'werewolves,' as the white men call them, were capable of many things, with their sharp claws and teeth and highly developed senses of sight, hearing and smell. They also use a strange white powder that paralyzes the victim."

"Is it in the DNA? Is it a genetic flaw?"

"According to Navaho folklore, it is not possible for a person to become a werewolf simply of their own choosing. The creatures act in obedience to hereditary traits and occult powers, which enable them to journey through the air and abandon themselves to cannibalism. It can also be a contagious condition which can be transmitted to anyone bitten by a werewolf."

Wolfe raised his eyebrows, then finished off his glass of gin.

Rachel continued, "A witch-owl must take certain precautions. She frees herself of her skin prior to flight, then hides the skin in a cool, dry place so that it will not shrink. For the werewolf to return to human form, she must recover her skin."

Remembering that he had promised to take Millie turtle-watching, Wolfe said, "Excuse me, Rachel, I've got to run. Millie and I are due on the beach to meet some old four-hundred-pound females about to go into labor." He paused. "I hesitated telling you, Rachel. Guzman's painting of Erzulie is missing."

"How dreadful," she said, shaken. Then she sighed and fell quiet.

"What is it, Rachel?" Wolfe asked.

"At my age, I don't remember things very well, but I remember a strange story about an Erzulie painting. I need to call my daughter Laurie to check some old correspondence. I'll let you know tomorrow."

...14

THE BEACH WAS PITCH DARK, except when the crescent moon peeked in and out behind the clouds. Wolfe sniffed the strong salt smells and heard the rhythmic throbbing of the surf. A mosquito whined past his ear.

"Be careful," Millie said. "Without a flashlight, you could fall."

"We can't use flashlights," Wolfe grumbled. "Sis said bright lights disorient the darling little hatchlings. Then they wander away from the ocean, get run over by cars on the highway, and it would be forever on our consciences."

"Why couldn't we watch turtles at a sensible hour?" Millie said. "When I ask you to walk with me, you're always too busy. But as soon as two strange women invite you for a walk at night on the beach, you get all excited."

Wolfe put his arm around Millie's shoulder. "Honey, this may be a once-in-a-lifetime experience, like the time I insisted you watch television when Tiger Woods played the final round of the U.S. Open. We may never again have the opportunity to watch loggerhead turtles laying eggs. They don't do it in daylight. How would you like to give birth with people in bathing suits standing around staring?"

"That's not even funny—"

Out of the darkness a surprised voice asked, "Who's there?"

"It's us, Sis, the Wolfes. We're here to watch turtles, remember?"

The two Bunting women conferred in hushed whispers. Then Toots said, "We're glad you decided to join us. Sis will explain everything."

"Loggerheads leave the water in the dark," Sis said, "and they crawl above the high tide line, about where we're standing. Then they dig holes with their rear flippers, deposit about a hundred ping-pong-ball-sized eggs, cover them with sand, and return to the ocean. The incubation period is roughly two months. It's rare to see hatchlings emerge and scurry to the water, but when you do, it's an incredible sight."

"How do we find the turtles?"

"Look for patterns of flipper marks in the sand."

"Yesterday," said Wolfe, "you said fifty thousand loggerhead nests were recorded each year in Florida. If each loggerhead lays one hundred eggs, that's five million per year; that's a hell of a lot of baby sea turtles."

"Only a small percentage of hatchlings survive. When the young turtles break out of their shells they head toward the brightest horizon, which normally is the reflective light of the ocean. But they're at high risk from pollution, beach lighting, and predator dogs or birds. In the sea, larger fish prey on them. Only one or two in a thousand survive. Even then, loggerheads still have enemies, like sharks and man."

"Man?" Millie asked.

"Loggerheads have existed for millions of years with little serious threat until now. Pollution, loss of nesting areas, and fish nets contribute to their decline. Ocean pollution and dumping are the worst problems. Many turtles die from eating plastics dumped in the ocean. Plastic looks like jellyfish, which turtles love to eat. Once ingested, the plastic blocks the intestines and causes death by starvation.

"Okay," Sis said, "let's get started. We only have an hour or so. Max, you go with Mother; I'll take Millie. We'll walk on the beach south for two hundred yards, then come back. You two start north."

"How can we see with no light?" Millie complained.

"Your eyes acclimate to the dark, and the partial moonlight will give us enough visibility."

Wolfe and Toots Bunting trudged along the shoreline looking for flipper-tracks or the huge, arched shells of four-hundred-pound turtles. The semidarkness made it difficult. They found no tracks, turtles, or little hatchlings scurrying to the water. After an hour of walking barefoot in the dry, soft sand and seeing nothing, Wolfe was bored and his calves ached. Only the squawk of the gulls disturbed the calm. He gazed out at the ocean and was surprised by three quick bursts of yellow light.

The night air was growing chilly. An owl screeched in the darkness. *Whaaa whaaaaaa-a-a-aark.* Wolfe smelled a damp, musky aroma. A rapid fluttering sounded overhead. For a moment the sky was lit by a burning brownish-white streak which forked crazily across the sky, trailing a luminous comet-like reflection in the moonlight. The hairs on the nape of his neck stirred. He felt a heavy splatter on his shoulder and thought, *Great, bird shit. That's all I need.*

"We should wrap it up, folks," Sis said. "It's late and we're all tired. I guess we've struck out tonight. Max, you and Millie go on in. Mother and I will take a stroll on the beach before retiring. Thanks for joining us. Good night."

"Did we just get the bum's rush from that girl?" Wolfe asked. "Millie, I'm sorry I dragged you out tonight for nothing."

"It was so dark I couldn't see," Millie whined. "But Sis could. She wore goggles."

"Goggles?"

"She said they were night vision glasses to help find the loggerheads."

Wolfe hosed the sand and tar off of their feet. "I saw signal lights coming off the ocean. Maybe it was just a buoy anchored in the channel."

"In spite of all that talk about bringing no lights," Millie said, "Sis took a flashlight out of her bag and pointed it out to sea. She said she was testing the batteries. I know I'm a Piscean, and you say I worry about everything, but could Sis and Toots be mixed up in something illegal?"

"You mean is sweet, turtle-saving, vegetarian-eating Sis Bunting into drug smuggling?"

"Something's not right," Millie insisted. "I have an eerie feeling about this place."

"Honey, you have a vivid imagination. Don't worry. Tomorrow will be interesting. Rachel thinks she may have the answer to Bernie's missing painting, and then we'll find out if Toots and Sis Bunting are international drug-runners. My immediate problem is that some bird shit on my shoulder and ruined my sport shirt."

Millie squinted at Wolfe in the dim light and gasped, "Max, that's not bird dropping. My God, it's *blood*!" Her eyes grew wide. "Sweetheart, are you all right?"

Wolfe brought his hand to his shoulder. His heart pounded. A ribbon of dark blood shone on his fingertips in the moonlight. "I didn't injure myself; the blood must have come from a bird."

The high-pitched caterwaul of a police siren pierced the late night stillness. Two more sirens joined the chorus. They saw flashes of intense blue pulsing strobes, and portable sodium vapor lights bathed the scene in a harsh white glow.

Millie yelled, "There's a crowd at the pool! Maybe somebody had a heart attack."

They hurried across the sand towards the lobby. The entire parking area was lit by pulsating police lights, casting bursts of red and blue light against the building.

"What's going on?" Wolfe demanded. He could see TV trucks arriving, vans with satellite uplinks, and he could hear the dull thud of a police helicopter circling the spa. The local press were pushing up against a yellow tape, arguing with police.

"Something happened to the old lady in 310," someone said.

"Rachel!" Wolfe cried out, rushing toward her room. "I'm a doctor," he shouted, forcing his way through police into the room. Rachel Walters lay on the floor, crumpled on her side, nearly naked. Her nightgown was slashed with jagged rents. A mass of crimson blood pooled beneath her head and chest. Wolfe could see a gaping red wound in her throat. Her flesh was a strange tallow color. The angle of her head and shoulders looked wrong. *Her neck is broken*, Wolfe thought. The sickly-sweet, coppery odor of blood made him dizzy. It was the expression on her face, a grimace of horror and pain, that forced Wolfe to look away. On the opposite wall he saw a crude blood-red drawing, scrawled in lines and circles.

The room was filling with crime scene technicians, police and detectives, and the impersonal noise of strangers: footsteps, orders, slamming dresser drawers, light bulbs flashing. Two paramedics emerged from the pack of onlookers with a white-sheeted gurney. The medical examiner was standing beside the bed, back turned, writing on a clip-board.

"Why would anyone murder Rachel?" Wolfe mumbled. The veins in his temple throbbed.

Millie appeared at Wolfe's side, speechless. Tears flowed freely down her cheeks. They watched as two men carried the gurney to the back of an ambulance and slid it inside. The door slammed, and some-one started the motor. The police barricades had been set up too late; rubberneckers were overrunning the beach and dune.

Each sob from Millie pressed on Wolfe's chest. He inhaled a deep breath, not sure what words were going to spill out. "No human would do what I saw," he said. "It was stomach turning. If I didn't know better, I'd say Rachel was murdered by some kind of wild ani-mal."

...15

"THIS IS STEVE KRASNER OF YOUR LOCAL CHANNEL FIVE NEWS TEAM. We are reporting the brutal slaying of a Vero Beach art dealer, Rachel Walters, at the Paradise Spa in Palm Beach. Channel Five's reporter Susan Smythe is on the scene. Good morning, Susie."

"It's not a good morning here at the Paradise Spa, Steve. Sometime around midnight a woman identified as Rachel Walters was killed in what appears to be a Voodoo-related death."

"What do you mean, Voodoo-related?" the anchor asked.

"Eyewitnesses report Mrs. Walters' room is a shambles, and a crude symbol was painted on the wall in red paint. Police have sealed off the area, and the medical examiner just left. He told me the time of death was approximately 11:15 p.m."

"How are the spa's guests reacting, Susie?"

"They're panicking and checking out in droves."

"Do police believe the crime is related to the Voodoo incident in Fort Pierce?"

"Palm Beach Sheriff Bunkie Trueheart is with me now. Sheriff, can you give us an update on the murder of Rachel Walters?"

"Well now," Trueheart proclaimed, smiling at the TV camera, "we have a significant lead. I anticipate making an arrest in the very near future."

"That's fast work, Sheriff. Back to you, Steve."

"This wraps up our special coverage of the apparent ritual slaying of a Vero Beach art dealer. Is this the beginning of a spree of Voodoo murders in Palm Beach County? Are your children safe on our streets? What lurks out there in the darkness? Stay tuned to Channel Five."

Wolfe couldn't sleep. He forced himself out of bed and, without disturbing Millie, he revisited the murder room. Rachel's door was open. Police and people in civilian clothes were still busy dusting and collecting evidence. Dresser drawers, books and clothing remained scattered on the floor. Wolfe stared again at the terrifying-looking symbol scrawled in red on the wall. He could see Rachel's blood soaked into the sheets and mattress. It was still stickily wet, and bits of bone and tissue were adhering to it. Anger coursed through him as he stumbled away from the room. He fought to tamp down his rage, his body trembling with adrenaline.

In the spa lobby, Wolfe eyed Charles Basil and seized his arm. "Come with me," he urged. "Maybe you can explain what the hell's going on."

Basil hesitated. "Best leave it to the police, Dr. Wolfe."

"They don't know jack-shit about Haiti. Come with me, Charles."

Reluctantly, Basil accompanied Wolfe to the crime scene. He gaped at the blood-red caballa-like symbol on the wall. "That's the *vévé* of a Haitian Petro cult," Basil said, shaken. "*Sect Rouge*, the Horrible Red Sect."

Wolfe studied the crude image. "What's the Horrible Red Sect?"

Basil was nervous. "I've heard of this in Haiti, but never in North America. Each Voodoo loa has a ritual symbol called a vévé. It's traced on the ground during a ceremony, and its purpose is to summon the spirit."

"You said it was a Haitian Petro cult?"

Basil was ashen. Wolfe picked up the tiny spark of fear in his eyes. Charles Basil's hands were shaking. "I need a drink," he whispered. "Come to my office."

Basil poured a glass of kleren for Wolfe and himself. "In Haiti there are two types of spirits—the *Rada* and the *Petro*. The Rada represent the old African traditions. They're benevolent. But conditions in the slave days in Haiti were harsh—anything but benevolent. In that severe environment developed the Petro society—a new kind of loa. The Petro pantheon of spirits is frightening, violent and dangerous."

Basil hesitated. "Few people in Haiti will talk about the Petro secret society. Haitians fear it as one of life's most hideous encounters. The *Sect Rouge*, or Red Sect, has a long tradition, and many say it still operates today. *Rouge* means 'red' in French, a word applied to this group because blood, human blood, is important in their rituals."

"You think this connects to Rachel's death?"

"The Sect Rouge practice human sacrifice," Basil said, refilling his glass. "Their meetings begin late at night at a dark, secluded place. Members are dressed in red and white robes, wearing straw hats with tall crowns. They hold candles and crack whips in the air as they move in a column to a crossroads, the favorite place for taking their victims. That is where they make the offering of food, drink, and money to Legba, Lord of the Crossroads. After that they go to a cemetery to make offerings to Baron Samedi, Lord of the Cemetery. The goal is to obtain a 'goat without horns,' a human being."

Wolfe felt the heat rise to his face. "You're talking—human sacrifice?"

Basil hesitated, then silently nodded. "They recite secret incantations over the victim, after which he is strangled. If you work in a Haitian hospital long enough, particularly one serving the rural population, you hear things about the secret societies and about the terror they invoke."

"Go on," Wolfe said impatiently.

"One night, I heard drums throbbing from the mountain behind the hospital. At first, I thought it was someone's boom box. The sounds didn't have the deep singing quality of the Rada drums. This was a high-pitched, repetitious sound. I was curious. I asked one of my young Haitian hospital residents to come with me. He said, 'Doc, that's a place you don't want to go. Don't ever search for the Petro drums. Some things are too dangerous to see.' I was curious, but I backed off."

"You did the right thing."

"Another time, I smelled an unpleasant odor outside my window and found the husband of one of my maternity patients burning something foul-smelling. I said, 'Mr. Calixte, what are you doing this late at night?' 'Doctor, I be driving off evil things,' he told me."

"What 'evil things'?"

" 'It's the *Cochon Gris*,' he said. 'The Gray Pigs who eat people are after my new baby son, and I am making the ritual ceremony to drive them off.' I calmed him down and invited him for coffee. He begged me not to be angry. He said, 'I cannot come in, doctor, until daylight, when the Cochon Gris are gone.' "

"This sounds like a Stephen King novel."

"No, the Cochon Gris were there. I looked out my window and saw maybe thirty people. They were holding candles in their hands. I heard the cracking of whips. They were marching in a straight column, like a military platoon. In the moonlight, I saw them, people in red and white gowns with conical hats. It was scary. I called security and they told me not to worry, that it was a local festival and I should stay indoors."

"What did you do?"

"I made rounds the next day, and Mrs. Calixte was sitting in bed nursing her new son. My fears of the night before seemed foolish. Then Calixte came into his wife's room and whispered to me that he had also seen figures in blood red gowns and hoods lurking around the hospital.

"I repeated the story to one of my Haitian colleagues, an anesthe-siologist who was educated at Columbia. He said, 'Our peasants are an imaginative lot. Their Creole metaphors could be misunderstood by people unfamiliar with their ways.' "

"Isn't that possible?"

Basil went on, "At dinner that evening, an American student doing volunteer work in the nursery told me she heard the anesthesiol-ogist screaming at Calixte, telling him he was a fool for discussing such things with foreigners who would go off and say bad things about Haiti. He said Calixte would be punished. The next day Calixte and his family were gone, with no explanation. I tried to locate the family to see how my patient and the baby were doing. When I got to their home, a funeral was in progress. 'Where's Mr. Calixte?' I asked a neighbor. The man said, 'A truck backed into him and crushed his head.' "

"Charles, you're a trained scientist. It's all circumstantial."

Basil stared hard at Wolfe. "You dragged me to Rachel's room. I saw the blood-red vévé. Secret societies, like the Horrible Red Sect, have existed in Haiti for centuries. Some people claim the Sect Rouge is dominated by criminals and psychopaths hiding behind the mask of Voodoo."

"But why would the Sect Rouge harm Rachel?" Wolfe asked.

"I don't know," Basil said in a low, hoarse voice. "When I iden-tified myself to the paramedics, they told me Rachel Walters was strangled before her neck was slashed."

"I'M FRIGHTENED," Millie said, throwing clothes into a suit-case.

"Calm down. Of course I want to leave this place, but we need to find out about Rachel's funeral arrangements first."

A grating voice on a bullhorn boomed: "We know you're in there, Wolfe. This is Sheriff Trueheart of the Palm Beach Sheriff's office. The area is surrounded. Snipers are on the roof. You have one minute to come out with your hands up!"

The Wolfes froze, wide-eyed, in shock and disbelief.

They heard somebody yell, "*Go! Go! Go!*" followed by a loud crack, as five grim-faced SWAT team members poured through the shattered door hollering, "Nobody move!"

Sheriff Trueheart strutted into the room, surveying the partly-packed luggage. "Getting ready to leave the scene of your crime? Looks like we got here in time."

A muffled cry escaped Wolfe's throat. "Are you out of your fucking mind?"

"Maxwell Wolfe, I arrest you for the murder of Rachel Walters."

"Oh my God!" Millie gasped

"Get me a lawyer," Wolfe said to Millie. "Call Perini and the Dorsett guy."

HANDCUFFED, WOLFE WAS LED out of the room by the barrel-chested, bullnecked sheriff. Standing in a semicircle of TV cameras, Trueheart addressed the crowd of onlookers. "Ladies and gentlemen, I'm pleased to report the apprehension of the killer of Rachel Walters. Palm Beach residents may now safely resume their normal lives."

Susan Smythe of Channel Five pushed her microphone in Trueheart's face. "Sheriff, could this be another mistaken arrest, like the Merriweather ladies?"

"Great gawdamighty, Susie, that was an honest mistake." The sheriff wiped his sweating brow. "We got this Wolfe man dead to rights."

"Did you say *wolfman*?" the reporter echoed loudly, knowing she would be making all the national networks tonight. "You mean the killer was a *werewolf*?"

"Huh?" Bunkie Trueheart stammered.

AT THE STATION HOUSE, Wolfe was ushered into a bleak gray-walled room.

"Mind if I record our conversation?" Trueheart asked. The sheriff produced a tape recorder and pushed the record button. No red light came on. "Testing, testing," Trueheart said, then hit the playback button. Nothing happened.

"Your batteries and brain are both dead," Wolfe observed dryly.

Trueheart glared. "Let's stop messing around. Where were you last night?"

"This is crazy. Last night Rachel Walters showed me a painting she got out west. Then my wife, Millie, and I met two women, the Buntings, on the beach to look for nesting loggerhead turtles. All these people can vouch for my whereabouts."

"Well, friend," Trueheart wheezed. "There's a little problem with your witnesses. The Bunting women checked out of the spa at two a.m. They paid in cash. Your fingerprints are in the victim's room, and you were the last person to see Mrs. Walters alive. Do I need to draw you a diagram, doctor?"

"You're setting yourself up for a major lawsuit, you idiot," Wolfe snapped.

Beads of sweat gathered on Trueheart's brow. The media were encamped in his office waiting for the promised confession. He needed results to launch his fading reelection bid.

"Because you're being uncooperative, Wolfe, I'm putting you in the holding tank. Maybe a little quality time with Big Luther will loosen your memory."

Wolfe was yanked to his feet by a guard and shoved into a cellblock with five other prisoners. A pungent aroma of urine, vomit and disinfectant permeated the cell.

Looking around the holding cell, Wolfe noticed a huge, bald, gator-faced black man, about six foot five, with bulging prison-gym muscles. The man had a nonchalant appearance, eyes partly closed. The giant noticed the newcomer. "How you doin'? You makin' it all right?"

Wolfe's scalp tightened.

"Best leave him be, Big Luther," warned one of the other prisoners. "He suppose to be a werewolf or some such shit."

Icy fear gripped Wolfe. He knew Trueheart wanted to terrify him into confessing.

The big man approached, his sleepy black eyes sunk beneath

thick brows. *I'm dead*, Wolfe thought. His head reached up to Big Luther's chest.

"I know you cool, man, but don't give me no attitude, okay?" Luther poked two fingers hard into Wolfe's chest. "You hear me talk to you, werewolf-man, or you deaf?"

Wolfe didn't know how to react. In panic, he raised his hands in front of his chest defensively, brushing hard against Big Luther's extended fingers. The towering man staggered, eyes rolling into the back of his head, jerking and shuddering in an uncontrollable spasm. Wolfe watched, astonished, as Big Luther's huge limbs shook violently. Foam flecked his mouth. Then Luther crumpled to the cell floor, unconscious. The other men in the cell pulled away in fright.

"I told him not to fuck with the Wolfman," a prisoner said, banging on the bars and yelling, "Hey guard! Get us out 'fore this white mo'fucka do us next!"

IN THE PALM BEACH COLUMBIA HOSPITAL emergency room, Big Luther awoke, attended by two guards from the sheriff's office. A young, overworked resident inquired with genuine concern, "Mr. Youngblood, are you feeling better?"

Big Luther stared around with vacant eyes. "Wha's happenin'?"

"You've just experienced a grand mal epileptic seizure, the result of a temporary disturbance of your brain impulses, an abnormal electrical charge, so to speak. It's like the static you might get on a radio. Medically it is called a cerebral dysrhythmia."

Big Luther looked up. "The fuck you talkin 'bout?"

...16

WEREWOLF MURDER SUSPECT ARRAIGNED

PALM BEACH POST. In what is being hailed as one of the most sensational crimes of the year, police in Palm Beach, Florida, arraigned an eighty-year-old Caucasian male, Maxwell Wolfe, a retired psychoanalyst, on suspicion of the brutal murder of a Vero Beach art dealer, Mrs. Rachel Walters.

Palm Beach Sheriff Bunkie Trueheart, in a televised press conference, is reported to have said that the man arraigned and held without bail is suspected of being a werewolf.

An unexplained Voodoo symbol was found scrawled on the wall in the deceased's hotel room. This is the second Voodoo-related incident in the South Florida area in two weeks.

Tourist businesses, already affected by the sluggish economy, are concerned that the Voodoo scare will discourage vacationers from coming to Florida this year.

The accused is being represented by Elvar T. Pfarr, a malpractice attorney. "Our firm is expanding," Pfarr said. "This will be my first criminal case."

...17

"YOU HAVE A VISITOR," the guard said, then edged cautiously back from the cell.

"Good morning, Dr. Wolfe," the man said, presenting his card. "My name is Elvar T. Pfarr. Your wife has engaged me to represent you in this legal unpleasantness."

Wolfe eyed the small, thin man with thick glasses and glossy dark hair combed straight back. *Good God!* he thought. *Peter Lorre is my attorney.*

Pfarr smiled his pleasant smile again and opened an imitation alligator briefcase. "As a New York State lawyer, I've received permission to be admitted to the jurisdiction of Florida under a motion of *pro hoc vice* to appear on your behalf. The case against you is serious."

"Serious? Tell me you're joking."

The lawyer continued, "I advanced, on your behalf, a contribution to the sheriff's reelection campaign. In exchange, I received a copy of the charges against you." Pfarr fumbled with his papers, squinting. "I think it reads that the prosecutor's going for first degree murder and reckless homicide. Unfortunately, your fingerprints are all over the crime scene, and you cannot verify your whereabouts at that time—"

Wolfe cut in. "I was with two women named Bunting. What would be my motive?"

"The police believe the motive was passion."

"Passion? Rachel was eighty-seven years old."

Pfarr referred again to his notes. "Supporting their case, the Paradise Spa's reflexologist, a Miss Jenine Greenfield, reported that she overheard you and the victim discussing sex. As a professional reflexologist, she will testify that from massaging your instep, she could tell you're a person with deeply repressed sadomasochistic sexual tendencies."

Wolfe chuckled. "My wife will be pleased to learn that."

The lawyer added, "The police are also aware of your involvement in another Voodoo-related unpleasantness in Fort Pierce. They think you had the means, motivation, and opportunity to murder poor Ms. Walters."

Wolfe stared hard at Pfarr. Their eyes met, and there was a thick silence in the room.

"I would like to review our defense strategy," Pfarr said. "We could employ the O. J. Defense, or as it is called in the trade, the 'Racial and Ethnic Defense Strategy.' "

"What the hell do I have to do with O. J. Simpson?" Wolfe snapped.

"The Simpson case was the most widely watched criminal proceeding in history. Simpson's lawyers accused the police of using nasty racial epithets, including the insulting *N-word*. The partially black jury deliberated for only a few hours before acquitting Simpson."

"So?"

"Words inspire attitudes, Dr. Wolfe. This trial is in Florida. There are a lot of old retired Jewish people living here who may be impaneled for jury duty. Jews will be grossly insulted if we can establish bias and anti-semitism. Did anyone use the... you know... the *K-word*?"

Wolfe gave a snort of amusement. "Trueheart's an asshole, not a racist."

Pfarr's voice faltered. "Too bad. Perhaps we can explore the Lorraine Bobbitt strategy, the 'Irresistible Impulse Defense.' You may remember that Lorraine Bobbitt is the lady who cut off her husband's penis because she said she was physically abused. An irresistible impulse forced her to perform a traumatic penectomy on Mr. Bobbitt. The jury found her temporarily insane at the time; she was acquitted and sent for a short time to a mental hospital."

Wolfe fought for composure. "I had no irresistible impulses."

Pfarr dug into his briefcase and took out a book. Thumbing through the pages, he paused. "We could always consider using the 'Adopted-Child Syndrome Defense.' Were you ever put up for adoption and never got over the trauma? You are now acting out your anger on an eighty-five-year-old motherly type like Rachel Walters."

"No. I was never adopted."

Pfarr mulled this over. "Next, let's consider the Menendez brothers strategy: 'I'm Insane, Don't Blame Me, Blame My Background Circumstances Defense.' You may have had a loss of self-control due to victimization and abuse. Did your father ever beat you?"

"Are you fucking out of your mind?"

Pfarr sighed, again looking through the legal textbook. "Here's the 'Urban Syndrome Defense.' Did you grow up in an area hemmed in by anti-semites and you believed you had to kill or be killed?"

Wolfe closed his eyes and lapsed into silence.

"Maybe we better stick to an insanity plea," Pfarr added thoughtfully. "The list of certified illnesses accepted by the American Psychiatric Association is over three hundred. We have to find the right one to make a jury believe you're nuts." He raised an amused eyebrow. "I'm reminded of a joke. You are a psychiatrist, right?"

"No, I was a psychologist."

"Anyway, did you hear the one about the guy who comes to a psychiatrist dressed in nothing but transparent Saran wrap? He says, 'Doc, what's the matter with me?' The psychiatrist looks at him and says, 'I can see your nuts.' "

Wolfe glared at his lawyer. "This is no time for stupid jokes. I shouldn't be in here. I'm innocent, goddamn it."

Pfarr took out a handkerchief to wipe his perspiring brow. "You must understand, Dr. Wolfe, that I'm a personal injury lawyer. This is my first murder trial, so please don't get testy."

THE FOLLOWING DAY, Pfarr brought Millie to visit. Wolfe eyed his wife curiously. "Why the hell did you die your hair blonde?"

"Max, you'll be proud of me. I'm restarting my singing career. Elvar is arranging for a New York publicist who will get me television and radio show interviews and an audition with Fremantle Media, one of the companies that produces *American Idol*. Isn't it exciting?"

Wolfe ran a shaky hand over his stubble and turned to Pfarr. "Instead of getting my wife on TV shows, why don't you go out and find the Bunting women who can prove I'm innocent?"

"Dr. Wolfe, the home address the Buntings used at the spa is an empty parking lot in North Miami. The ladies paid their bill in cash and departed at two a.m. Millie cannot testify for you, because there was a thirty-minute stretch when she was with the Bunting daughter, while you were alone at the time of the murder with an eyewitness who has completely vanished."

"BAD LUCK SEEMS TO AGREE WITH YOU, DR. WOLFE," Chief Perini said, winking at Preston Dorsett. "I love the decor. Are these walls painted the new Ralph Lauren Electric Chair Gray?"

"I've lost my sense of humor," Wolfe said. "This is like a Kafka novel. I'm arrested by a mentally-challenged, politically ambitious, publicity-seeking sheriff. I've got a dysfunctional malpractice attorney with the personality of warm spit, handling his first criminal case. I've got a wife who has dyed her hair and can't wait to get on *American Idol*, and you're making jokes."

"Not to worry, Dr. Wolfe," Dorsett said. "We'll sort this out."

"What's happening with the Guzman case?" Wolfe asked Perini.

"According to Dorsett, it would be much simpler if we were in Haiti; their penal code classifies zombification as murder, even when the victim is alive. It isn't that way in Fort Pierce. Without a body, we have no homicide. Bernard Guzman is still a missing person. But you have enough on your own plate. I understand that your eyewitnesses split."

"I'm really confused," Wolfe admitted. "These two nice ladies from the spa invited Millie and me to watch turtles crawl around the beach at night, because that's the best time to see the loggerheads. My lawyer says they left the spa at two a.m. and their home address is phony."

Chief Perini reflected, rubbing his palms together. "Why would two respectable women leave the spa in the middle of the night and give false identification? Tell me again, Max, exactly what were you doing on that beach?"

"We walked around looking for flipper tracks and had no luck. Then Sis Bunting said we should call it a night."

"Were your friends carrying any equipment?"

"It was pretty dark. Millie said Sis used night-vision goggles to locate turtle tracks—"

Dorsett interrupted. "Goggles. Anything else?"

"And Sis tested a flashlight."

Dorsett sighed. "If you had stayed on the beach another hour, you would have witnessed drugs or Haitian refugees coming ashore. The lady was using infrared monocular night vision glasses, either Bens 930 or a Jaguar night scope. With that equipment she could see in the dark."

"No way. These were decent women."

"We've had an increase in both drug-running and the number of Haitians smuggled in. Most smugglers treat the Haitians like animals. Your friends used night-vision equipment and a GPS receiver to make certain the boats had arrived offshore as scheduled."

"What happens after boat-people come ashore?"

"My guess is the Haitians were driven by your two lady friends in a closed truck to North Miami to be integrated into the local Haitian community there."

Perini said, "Your wife suggested I visit the Paradise Spa and to talk to a Dr. Charles Basil. She sensed Basil and the Bunting girl had something going."

"If you can locate the Bunting women, and if they vouch for my whereabouts, would they be facing any charges?"

"If two turtle-watchers check out early from a spa, there ain't no law against it."

"THE SECT ROUGE SYMBOL WAS A DIVERSION to frighten people and confuse the police," Lionel Beauvoir said as he visited in Wolfe's cell. The houngan's face darkened, but his voice remained calm. "No Petro Society would ever harm an innocent person, a *blanc* yet."

"I'm not naive, Lionel. We both know that secret societies exist in Haiti." He paused. "And, for all I know, maybe here too."

They sat in silence that wasn't cordial.

Lionel's face clouded over. "America has its hoodlum street gangs and its secret society, the Mafia. In Haiti, secret societies like the Sect Rouge and Cochon Gris are outlawed and hated by everyone."

Wolfe gave a short, mirthless laugh, glancing around the cell. "I have more to worry about than crazy Haitian cults. I'm sure this isn't a pastoral visit, Lionel. Why are you really here?"

He felt the intensity in the Voodoo priest's eyes as Lionel answered, "Haitian tourism and Haitian refugee policies will suffer from the unearned and unwanted publicity following the poor woman's murder. Washington politicians will have a good excuse to put needed aid programs on hold. We don't have an army of lobbyists. The lurid stories of loup garous and werewolves mean higher ratings for the networks and good copy for struggling newspapers—even if none of it is true."

"Since you're so forthcoming, Lionel, I'm curious. What's a loup garou?"

"In Haitian folklore there is a legend about a devil-witch, a loup garou. In English, it's werewolf. A loup garou is an evil person, mostly a female who sheds her skin and changes into an owl, flying about at night preying on humans. If she can't get back into her skin, she dies."

"You're a college physics teacher, Lionel? How can you believe such nonsense?"

"When Galileo discovered the moons of Jupiter, the astronomers of his time didn't take him seriously. They also called it nonsense, because the existence of these moons conflicted with their accepted beliefs. That's the way it's always been; people keeping their eyes and minds tightly shut when faced with new realities."

Wolfe looked into Lionel's dark, unblinking eyes as the houngan continued, "The reason I am here is that you are connected to Police Chief Perini and Josi's friend, Dorsett, of the FBI. They *must* understand that the murder at the spa was not committed by a Petro society. As a houngan, I know from experience that most nonpolitical murders are caused by sex or money. Mrs. Walters was an old lady, so it wasn't sex. She was an art dealer, so if money is involved, art is involved. There is a Creole expression: 'Money kills more than do knives.' "

"Thanks for sharing that quaint Creole homily, but I've got a slight problem. I'm in a goddamn jail cell, man. How can I help you or anyone else?"

The Voodoo priest's gray eyes dimmed to near black. He stood and clasped Wolfe's forehead tightly between both palms. "*Atibo-Legba,*" he chanted softly. "*By the power of Legba Atibon, guardian of the crossroads, Legba, guardian of the bush, Legba, guardian of the persecuted, Ago, Ago, si, Ago la. L'uvri bayé pu mwé, agoé. Pu mwé pas'!*"

Wolfe exhaled impatiently. "Lionel, please take your mumbo-jumbo and go away."

...18

SHERIFF BUNKIE TRUEHEART RESIGNS

PALM BEACH POST. City auditors took control of Sherriff Bunkie Trueheart's personal bank accounts, totaling eight million dollars, which had been illegally transferred from collected parking fines, speeding tickets, and campaign contributions.

A spokesman for Sheriff Trueheart said that the sheriff's department was "short-staffed and a little behind in their paperwork."

Trueheart announced his retirement, claiming that he needed to spend more time with his family.

In a related matter, Palm Beach Police released from custody the man accused of the grisly murder of Vero art dealer Rachel Walters. His release was based upon the late appearance of two witnesses who volunteered testimony, under oath, that they were with the suspect, Maxwell Wolfe, at the time of the murder at the Paradise Spa.

...19

A SHADOW CROSSED MILLIE'S FACE. "Are you trying to kill yourself?" she said in bewilderment and frustration. "Max, you've been in jail, eating that garbage. You have a heart condition. You're no kid. Instead of coming home and resting, now you want to visit an art gallery in Palm Beach. You're *farmish*?"

Wolfe murmured, "The food wasn't so bad."

"Wonderful! Prison food is better than mine. Maybe I can get their recipes."

"Honey, calm down, please. While we're in the Palm Beach area, I want to check out the other dealer who bid on Bernie's art collection. They're making no progress on Rachel's murder. It's the least I can do."

Millie looked at him, started to say something, and then only shook her head as they approached a rundown-looking storefront on the corner of 8th street and US 1. The chipped and cracked sign read: "House of Valdesi. Unusual Arts and Objects."

In contrast to the sunny afternoon heat, the store interior was cool and darkened. Wolfe detected a faint moldy odor. Behind the counter, they eyed a thickset man with a drooping mustache, cold eyes, and a wiry mane of gray-streaked hair pulled back into a ponytail.

"Mr. Valdesi?"

The man shot them a look of irritation, but didn't reply.

"My name is Dr. Wolfe, and this is my wife, Millie. Rachel Walters mentioned your interest in Bernard Guzman's art collection."

Valdesi's eye's flashed briefly; then he said flatly, "What business is that of yours?"

Wolfe felt a wave of anger wash over him. "Rachel was my friend; I'm making it *my* business." He took out his cell phone, scrolled down to Dorsett's number, and leaned forward, letting the barely controlled anger flood into his voice. "Either talk to me, or talk to the FBI."

Valdesi stiffened and was briefly silent. He gave a short, mirthless laugh. "Sorry if I came off rude. It's been a hectic day."

Wolfe said, "Rachel mentioned that you spend a lot of time in Haiti."

"When you deal in Haitian art, you've got to be on the scene. Poverty is rampant. Even when you have signed contracts for artwork, if an artist finishes a piece and somebody comes along with hard cash, poof, it's gone. For years I've kept an apartment in Petionville. I live there part of the year to insure my supply of paintings and sculptures."

Glancing around, Wolfe commented, "For a retailer, you carry little inventory."

"Most artwork for my clientele is custom-ordered. My specialty area is occult art."

Millie pointed to a tablet of a large animal with a human face. "What is that?"

"Thousands of years ago people scratched drawings on cave walls. Cro-Magnon animal paintings and carvings were found in caves in Europe. This is a statue of the *Sorcerer of Trois Freres*, a sixteen-thousand-year-old carving of an animal-human hybrid, found near Ariége in the French Pyrénées. The body is a large animal with the ears and horns of a stag, the tail of a wolf, and the legs of a dancing shaman. The sorcerer symbolizes animal-human fusions."

Millie sighed. "It's frightening."

"Have you ever heard of skinshifters?" Wolfe asked.

"Yeah, the Navaho witches that change into animals. Myths about shapeshifting creatures persist worldwide. In South America, the *chonchon* is a witch that changes into a big bird. Look." Valdesi rummaged through a file and withdrew an old photograph of a man in costume.

"Legend has it that the *chonchon* has the shape of a human head with devil horns and extremely large wings for flying on moonless nights."

Wolfe snickered. "To me, the werewolf, vampire literature and films are being foisted on a public hungry to fantasize about creatures who are everything that they are not: charismatic, seductive, and immortal. It is superstition-pandering for profit."

"No question, vampires are popular today," Valdesi admitted. "However, the most widely held superstition throughout the world is the belief in the werewolf, or lycanthrope."

"You're not about to serve up some supernatural crap on me, are you?" Wolfe asked.

Valdesi shrugged, "Believe what you will. I am a student of lycanthropy—from the Greek word *lykoi*, or wolf, and *antropos*, meaning man. From my analysis of Internet blogs, millions of people are intrigued with the notion that werewolves are humans that change

into animal form during certain lunar aspects." He rubbed his hands together. "In this miserable economy, the more people who believe in vampires and werewolves and want to collect occult art, the better."

Valdesi showed the Wolfes a sequined flag.

Millie gasped. "What on earth?"

"This flag portrays a female loup garou, a Haitian werewolf who sheds her skin, changes into a bird, and strangles then sucks the blood of her victims. When she's in flight, a luminous trail marks the loup garou's track through the sky. These look like comets and are called werewolf clusters, or *nids de loups-garous*."

That's what I saw on the beach, Wolfe thought.

"In the archipelagic state of Trinidad," Valdesi added, "the loup-garou is called a *lugarhoo*. In West Africa, they are called *succetts* or suckers, or as we would say—vampires."

"How do people become werewolves?" Millie asked.

"It's hereditary—a genetic trait. There have been reports of individuals becoming infected after being bitten by a male or female loup garou, through the blood, like hepatitis—"

"And, they turn into vampires, right?" Wolfe cut in, laughing. "Who is this cute fellow?"

"This is a Haitian *zobop* by the artist George Liautaud. His material comes from steel drums. Liautaud cuts the sheets in half, flattens them, then transfers the patterns to the metal with chalk. Using chisels, dies and a hammer, he cuts and molds the designs. His work is in the Museum of Modern Art in New York."

"Museum of Modern Art," Wolfe echoed. "That's impressive. What *is* a *zobop*?"

Valdesi's voice abruptly sobered. "A hairless pig," he said. "Only with reluctance will rural Haitians go out alone at night. What they fear is to encounter groups of hairless pigs, called the cochon gris. Zobops have a nasty reputation for eating people.

"But not every-thing is grim." He directed their attention to another metal work. "Here is the *Modern Vampire*, by Murat Brierre. The artist told me that he was inspired to create this piece of sculpture because neighbors told him about a young woman, living right in the neighborhood, who was thought to be a particularly vicious loup garou; she traveled around at night by bicycle rather than flying. When I asked the artist what he meant to represent, he

laughed and said that it was a humorous testament to the adaptability of Haitians to modern times.'"

Wolfe felt a sense of foreboding beneath Valdesi's air of confidence and attempted good humor. Changing the subject, he asked, "Did you ever see Bernard Guzman's collection?"

"Yeah," the man answered guardedly.

"What did you think about the Erzulie painting by Hyppolite?"

"Nice picture," Valdesi said, narrowing his eyes. "So?"

"So. I think you know that the missing Erzulie is connected to Rachel's murder."

After an awkward silence, Valdesi emitted a short laugh. "Thanks for stopping by."

"DIDN'T YOU SEE THE NO-LOITERING SIGN outside the police station?" Perini complained. "If it wasn't for druggies, murderers, bank robbers, and zombies wandering Fort Pierce, every day would be Christmas. What do you want? I'm busy."

"That Valdesi fellow had a sleazy look," Wolfe replied. "I think he could be complicit in the Walters murder. He was competing with Rachel Walters to handle the sale of Guzman's collection. There's motive, opportunity, and—"

"And nothing," Perini cut in. With his elbows on his desk, he steepled his fingers and said, "I'm not involved in the spa murder case. It's out of my jurisdiction. As a professional courtesy, the new Palm Beach sheriff advised me that Valdesi was in a bar with witnesses watching a Marlins game at the time of the murder. Satisfied?"

Wolfe ignored Perini's comment. "I also think Phillipe Louissant is involved in this mess. Did you check *his* whereabouts the night of the murder?"

"You're on the wrong track, Wolfe," Perini interrupted. "Louissant also has an ironclad alibi. He was in front of twenty students in a night-school course in Orlando. I doubt he could be in two places at the same time—unless he can fly. We had his identity checked through the computers. The official version is that Louissant and his mother escaped Haiti in 1986, claiming political refugee status during the turmoil there. Prior to that, there is no information. Zilch."

"Isn't it possible he and his mother could have taken on new identities? With money, it couldn't be hard to get credit cards, phony passports and driver's licenses."

Perini softened. "I know you're taking this murder case personally, but you've got to let it go. You're eccentric, but you're not Monk, and this isn't TV. In the real world, unfortunately, we don't win 'em all."

"There are still loose ends," Wolfe persisted. "I'm going to Vero Beach to meet Rachel's daughter. She has letters she wants me to see. Before I go, I want to thank you for contacting Charles Basil. The Bunting women came forward and vouched for me. It was a lifesaver."

Perini shrugged. "I never reached the spa doc. He had already left for Haiti."

Then how the hell did the Buntings—? Wolfe had an uncomfortable premonition.

...20

WOLFE'S EYES TOOK IN THE TIDY WHITE CLAP-BOARD BUILDING housing the Galerié Louverture. Walking in, he saw a small office and two large, sunlit gallery rooms filled floor-to-ceiling with Haitian paintings, Voodoo flags, and wall hangings.

An overweight young woman with a pretty face and long brown hair approached. "You must be Mom's friend, Dr. Wolfe. I'm Laurie."

"I'm deeply sorry about your mother's death."

"Every time I think of her, I burst into tears." Laurie wiped her reddened eyes and exhaled. "You want to look over her letter from Haiti, but first let me show you our gallery. We carry a cross-section of Voodoo artists. Here is one by Paléus Vital. His paintings are set in dark caves or dense jungles where secret Petro Society rituals take place. In Haitian art, the five-pointed star is a symbol of Africa, but notice this painting contains a six-pointed star."

"It looks like the Star of David," Wolfe said, fascinated. "And the writing says 'Adonai,' which is a Hebrew word meaning Lord. What does it signify?"

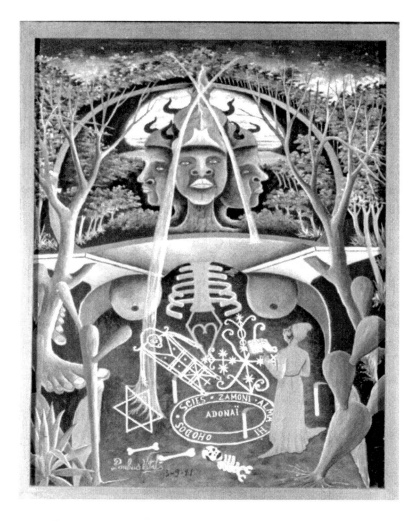

"Welcome to Voodoo art," Laurie said, turning to point out another work. "This painting is entitled *Phantom of the Night*, by Edgar Jean–Baptiste. It's on loan from the Yale University Art Gallery. In the painting Satan is depicted as the dark Petro side of the loa Legba towering over a street that goes to a vanishing point between his outstretched legs."

"Haiti seems to be well-stocked with malevolent demons," Wolfe said. "The hairless pigs, the zobops, Petro Legbas and loup garous."

"You *have* heard of loup garous?" asked Laurie. "We have a painting of one by Salnave Philippe-August. It is entitled *Anger*. Notice how the woman's hair turns into snakes, fangs grow out of her mouth, a snake entwines itself around the woman, and wings grow out of her back, typical of a Haitian werewolf."

Wolfe shook his head. "It amazes me how much Haitian art is fueled by superstition." He eyed a metal sculpture in a corner.

"This piece is by George Liautat," Laurie said. "In traditional voodoo iconography, Ogou represents the loa of war. The metal cut-out could be Liautat's visualization of a spirit possession during a Voodoo ceremony when a devotee is 'mounted' by a loa."

"I remember seeing Hyppolite's painting of Ogou in Bernard Guzman's apartment."

"Ogou is a very violent Voodoo spirit," Laurie said. "I have heard my Haitian artists say that when one is mounted in a trance by Ogou, the possessed person has to be very strong to harbor this spirit."

"Oh. Oh," Wolfe said, noticing a painting of a large owl and a strange-looking woman.

"This is Roger François' *Owl and Woman,*" Laurie said. "The metamorphosis of a loup garou, a woman transformed into a bird. Notice the claw-like hands."

Wolfe thought, *Guzman's nightmare: the huge bird, with talons like the paws of a mountain lion, perched on a half-naked Haitian woman smoking a cigarette.*

"Where did this painting come from?" Wolfe asked.

"Mother purchased it years ago from an old Haitian woman living in Fort Pierce. Here are the letters. Forgive me if I leave you alone. If you want coffee, just holler."

Wolfe glanced back at the foreboding owl with its malevolent eyes. An involuntary shudder rippled through him like an electric current. Opening the packet of Rachel Walters' correspondence, Wolfe scanned the yellowing pages. Two letters attracted Wolfe's interest.

Centre D'Art
15, Rue de Révolution
Port-Au-Prince, Haiti
August 14, 1948

Dear Rachel:

I'm sorry to advise you of the death of our dear friend Hector Hyppolite. What a tragic ending to a brilliant career. He died of a heart attack last week.

I still picture Hector the day we met him, dressed in striped pajamas. His features seemed more Indian than African; maybe he was descended from one of those Arawak sand painters who inspired the veves?

Sorry to bring you the bad news of Hector's death. Maybe that's why I'm feeling depressed. He stopped by last week to show me his latest work, a marvelous painting of Erzulie. It was glorious, his dark nude Maitresse Loa walking in a garden surrounded by birds and flowers. Hyppolite was presenting the painting to a young Haitian doctor named François Duvalier, who is using penicillin to heal cane workers' cuts. I shall miss Hector Hyppolite.

I look forward to visiting with you when I come back to the states.

Fondly,
Dewitt

119

The second letter was dated twelve years later.

Phoebe Stanton

July 23, 1960

Dearest Rachel,

Ira and I have come to the conclusion we must leave Haiti. The situation has deteriorated under Duvalier. We were foolish. We saw the signs: the graffiti, the attacks on the electoral offices. The evidence was there, but we kept hoping things would improve.

The mood is depressing. A newspaper friend told us Duvalier and his family are plundering the country. The stolen money is funneled to offshore banks by the Leopold woman who runs Duvalier's Tonton Macoute. We hoped for a democratic solution, but Duvalier is entrenched in the cities and countryside. The people think he is a Voodoo priest. With the Macoutes, he has his own army; there is no hope of democracy. As they say here: "Bilten se papse, bayonét se fé—the ballot is made of paper, but the bayonet is made of iron."

The final straw was last Wednesday. Joseph Martia was murdered. You may remember him. Joseph was the framer who did most of the work for the Musée d'Art. His wife, Theo, said someone from Duvalier's palace, the White House, gave him a Hyppolite painting to frame, with instructions for a special backing. When it was completed, Tonton Macoutes came to the house, took the painting and shot Joseph in the head. What a terrible tragedy.

Ira has been offered a job as the foreign affairs editor for the Baltimore Sun. When we get settled, we will motor down for a visit.

Love,

Phoebe

PART III

THE CROSSROAD

Kalfou pi pasé gran chémin.

The crossroad is older than the main road.

...21

"I'M BORED! What do I have to look forward to in life? *Nothing*, that's what," Millie grumbled. "I thought when you retired we would finally have time together, but no, you run around all day playing detective, then you're too tired to go out. When was the last time you took me dancing? I can't live like this anymore."

"Maybe you should see someone. Does your AFTRA health plan pay for—"

"I don't need a psychiatrist, thank you very much. I need excitement. Maybe I'll have a dinner party: Toots Bunting from the spa and that police chief. He and Toots will hit it off well. I want Mr. Pfarr to come; he'll like Wanda, and I'll invite Josi to bring the FBI person."

"Uh-huh."

"I want Josi's grandmother, Tata, to come because she had us to her house for dinner, but she probably won't be able to. She works part-time at Bahama Mama's Restaurant."

"Whatever," Wolfe answered, then looked up from his crossword puzzle. "What did you just say about Josi's grandmother?"

"Tata is the cook at Bahama Mama's Restaurant."

"*Bingo*," Wolfe whispered.

"THANKS FOR COMING EARLY," Wolfe said to Josi Beauvoir and Preston Dorsett. He shepherded them into the den and fixed drinks. "We need to talk. I don't want to upset you, Josi, but you're involved in a dangerous situation—"

"What are you talking about?" Dorsett interrupted.

"The photograph in Guzman's apartment. You spotted it while you were cleaning."

"Go on," Josi said, glaring at Wolfe.

"You recognized the woman in the picture, and you were

shocked. Then you took it home to show your grandmother. Tata confirmed that she was your mother, Jacqui, and the man was your real father—Bernard Guzman. Tata didn't know Guzman lived in the Fort Pierce area. I'm sure she was enraged."

"So, she borrowed a photograph. What's the big deal?" Preston asked.

Wolfe continued, "Guzman's behavior to your mother was unspeakable. He sent her back to Saut d'Eau because she wouldn't have an abortion. At the birth, your mother was attended only by Tata. You were a breech baby, Josi. Your mother died in childbirth. Guzman bears moral responsibility for her death. Had you been born in Port-au-Prince, the doctors would have performed a Caesarean delivery and your mother would still be alive."

"How do you know this?" Josi snapped, her eyes blazing.

"Guzman's name showed up on government computers because of his problems with the FDA. The computers registered anything in Haiti with his name. It appeared on a birth certificate in Saut d'Eau."

Josi breathed deeply, trying to suppress her nervousness. "Where is this leading?"

"It's understandable that you and Tata hated the man responsible for your mother's death. On the morning you found him gasping for breath on the floor of his unit and called 911, you removed the Hyppolite painting of Erzulie, Tata's special loa."

"The man caused my mother's death. I hated him, but not enough to kill him."

"But you know who does hate him enough to kill him."

"Be careful who you are accusing," warned Dorsett.

"I'm relating what happened. Chief Perini told me Guzman ate Tuesday night at Bahama Mama's Restaurant. When it comes to murder, I don't believe in coincidences. Tata cooks at Bahama Mama's. Guzman's waiter said he ordered conch chowder—Tata's specialty. Within hours after eating the chowder, Guzman was in a life-threatening coma."

"What proof do you have?"

"None. The restaurant can't be held accountable, because the chowder is prepared in batches. Hundreds of patrons ate conch chowder in Bahama Mama's on Tuesday and Wednesday. No one else reported being ill. The fact that Tata doctored the chowder would be impossible to prove. Plus, he isn't dead, he's missing."

Josi ran her fingers through her hair. "Preston, do I need a lawyer?"

Wolfe smiled. "Yes, but not to defend you."

"What the hell are you talking about?" Dorsett said.

"Guzman was Josi's legal father. With no other family, she is the only living relative. A lawyer can petition the court to appoint her guardian with authority to manage Guzman's assets until he's declared dead or found. The Hyppolite painting of Erzulie is legally yours. But a tragic, cold-blooded murder has been committed to obtain that painting. Please trust me with it for a while."

Turning to Dorsett, Wolfe said, "Preston, you know Louissant. Ask him a few bullshit questions about the murder, like 'Are there any physical characteristics of Sect Rouge murders that I can input into FBI and Interpol computers for similar MO's?' Mention that Josi is Guzman's real daughter and legal heir. He loaned his daughter the missing Erzulie painting for a Voodoo ceremony her grandmother was conducting. Explain that Josi has authorized me to dispose of Guzman's entire art collection. Then get back to me."

"Will do," said Dorsett.

"Is there anything I can do, Dr. Wolfe?" Josi asked

"When is Tata having her next Voodoo ceremony?"

"On Erzulie's birthday in three days."

"Can I get an invitation?"

"Of course. Anything else?"

"Let me borrow the Hyppolite painting."

"Isn't it also dangerous for you to have the Hyppolite?" Dorsett asked skeptically.

"Why would anyone kill for a painting they can purchase for a fraction of its real value? Don't worry, Louissant will call me."

"WANDA, SAY HELLO TO ELVAR PFARR," Millie said. "And you know Chief Perini. Everyone say hi to Toots Bunting," she continued. "We met Toots at the spa in Palm Beach. And this beautiful young lady is our darling friend, Josi Beauvoir, with the FBI man."

"Toots," Wolfe asked. "Can I talk to you privately for a moment?"

The woman nodded, eyeing Wolfe curiously.

"Thanks for clearing me with the Palm Beach police," he said. "Please satisfy my curiosity. What made you contact them?"

"Strange you should ask, Max. Sis and I were out on our boat, with no television. Sis woke up having a nightmare about you. She checked her laptop and found out about your ridiculous arrest. We headed back to the marina in Fort Lauderdale and contacted the authorities—"

Perini cut in. "She's my date, Wolfe. Find one of your own." Turning to Toots, he said, "What do you do for fun?"

"My late husband, Frank, was an avid fisherman. We had a forty-seven-foot Chris-Craft Commander and worked the major tournaments: January the Billfish Invitational out of Fort Pierce City Marina, then February down to Islamorada for the Women's Sailfish Tournament—"

Perini felt a tingle of surprise. "Hold on—do my ears hear you're a gen-u-ine fishing person, or did your hubby bait your line for you and take off the fish while you sat there sipping margaritas and looking pretty?"

"Bait my line, your ass, sailor."

Perini put his right hand over his heart. "Wolfe," he yelled. "I'm in love; this girl fishes."

Josi's and Dorsett's fingertips brushed under the table. Elvar Pfarr and Wanda Smeltzer were in deep conversation. Wanda's cello-playing fingers strummed Pfarr's left testicle.

"May I say grace?" Wanda asked, withdrawing her fingers from Pfarr's crotch. "Everyone please hold hands. Max, dear, lower the lights?"

"Are you saying grace or holding a seance?"

"Dear God," intoned Wanda. "We thank you for this food and all Thy blessings, and we pray Americans will stop being ethnocentric about nudity and accept this gentle source of freedom."

"And I say an amen to that, Madame," uttered Elvar T. Pfarr, as his penis returned to its normal flaccid state.

Wanda swigged her wine. "I can't understand how we can view Europe with its nude beaches, fewer teen pregnancies and less sex crimes and not understand the correlation. It is liberating to swim and sunbathe without a wet rag clinging to you."

Perini whispered to Toots, "Sounds like a good idea to me."

"Thanks anyway, honey, but I'm not the clothing-optional type."

Wanda asked, "Is Rosh Hashanah the holiday you light the eight candles?"

"No. That's Hanukkah."

"Well, which one is it you eat the unleavened bread?"

"That's Passover," Millie said. "Rosh Hashanah is when we blow our shofars."

"That's what I like about you Jews; you're so good to your help."

"What did she say?" Millie whispered to Max.

"Skip it."

Millie served the first course: chicken soup with matzo balls.

Pfarr tasted the broth. "Delicious. They say chicken soup is good for your health."

"Not if you're the chicken." Toots chuckled.

"Chicken soup is called Jewish penicillin," Wolfe explained. "It inhibits the clumping of certain white blood cells called neutrophils that cause congestion and inflammation in people suffering from the common cold."

"And the matzo balls," Perini added, "are a prescription for severe indigestion."

"Are you talking about these cute little round yellow things in my soup?" Wanda asked, winking at Elvar Pfarr. "The matzo balls are delicious. Are there any other parts of the matzo you can eat?"

Perini polished off his fourth glass of wine. He pressed his arm familiarly around Toots' shoulder. "I understand you like to watch turtles and hang out on beaches—late at night?"

She stiffened. "You want to know why?" she said. "Some years ago my husband Frank and I were fishing near one of the deserted is-lands in the Bahamas, Flamingo Key. At dusk, I spotted the hull of a sunken sailboat and a dozen people staggering across the sand, waving to us with their hands and shirts. Frank got the dinghy and his gun and we went ashore."

"What did you find?" Millie asked.

Everyone at the table stopped talking and listened to Toots relate her experience.

"There were dead bodies awash in the surf and fifty people suffering from dehydration."

"Bad scene," Perini commented, shaking his head.

"Most of the folks could barely swallow. I held one pregnant woman's head while Frank poured water in her mouth. We reached the Coast Guard by satellite phone; they said it would be hours before the nearest helicopter could get to us from Nassau station four hundred miles away. We lighted fires on the beach and waited. The first Coast Guard helicopter could only carry eleven people. Frank and I had to select them, then decide which four among the sickest remaining would get IV's."

"How dreadful," Josi said.

"We ministered to the Haitians until the Coast Guard helicopters arrived with food and medical supplies. The good news is the fifty Haitians all recovered. The bad news is the Bahamian authorities returned them all to Haiti. Since my husband died, my daughter Inez and I try to help Haitian refugees escape, any way we can."

Dorsett and Perini glanced at each other, but remained silent.

After Millie served coffee, the guests prepared to leave.

"How about an after-dinner drink in my apartment?" Wanda asked Pfarr.

Josi and Dorsett said their farewells and hurried out.

Toots Bunting glanced anxiously at her watch. "I've got to run." She pinched Perini's cheek and said, "Call me sometime, big boy."

The Fort Pierce police chief blushed and was speechless.

"WOULD YOU LIKE TO STOP FOR A NIGHTCAP?" Dorsett said quietly.

Josi responded with a slight lift of her eyebrows. "Do you have to drive all the way back to Miami tonight? It's late. Sleep at our house."

He could smell her hair, fragrant as fresh-cut herbs. "I already have a motel reservation, thanks," he said, stammering. "I don't fancy your overprotective grandmother getting mad and casting a magic spell on me. I could end up being sacrificed to your gods, or loa, or spirits, or whatever you call them. Your ceremonies do include sacrifices, don't they?"

She snickered, rolled her eyes and said, "Animal sacrifice is the climax of a Haitian Voodoo ceremony. Poultry, pigs, and goats are sold live in the rural markets. People are accustomed to seeing animals killed."

"Yuck. Sounds barbaric."

"Many religions use animal sacrifice. You don't see anything unusual on Thanksgiving for a turkey to be killed, and then at the table everyone says a prayer. In Voodoo we say a prayer first and then kill the animal. What's the difference?"

Dorsett smiled grimly. "But drinking blood—"

"Drinking blood is traditional. Don't Catholics go to church for communion and drink wine representing the blood of Christ?"

"But that's not real blood, it's only symbolic."

"Voodoo's an earthy religion. Some people say Haitians are barbaric for sacrificing animals, but how about people who eat veal? It's not on the menu as 'baby cow,' it's 'veal scaloppini.' They give it another name so we don't feel ashamed ordering it. Veal calves are raised in 22-inch wooden crates. This is how these sweet baby cows live their entire lives, chained by the neck, side by side, not allowed to walk or even turn around in their confinement. Can you imagine how terrible their little lives are? Who is inhumane?"

He raised his muscular hands in surrender. "I'm sorry I mentioned sacrifices."

She blushed slightly. "Preston, you once asked if I had ever experienced possession. I said that I didn't know you well enough to discuss it. I feel differently now. More trusting."

Dorsett gazed fondly at Josi's large, mischievous eyes, high cheekbones, and slightly upturned nose.

"Possession is called the *White Darkness*," she continued. "First, you just dance with the music of the polyrhythmic Rada drums and enjoy the liberating feeling. Voodoo drum beats are like the powerful vibrations of American hard rock music." She gave a shaky laugh. "The first time I was possessed, I danced until I was exhausted. The music was jarring, but exciting. My left foot suddenly became rooted to the floor. It frightened me and I tried to pull backward, falling into some people's arms. They must have pushed me back on the floor, because I was dancing once more until the leg again stuck in place. There was an unpleasant dizziness in my head, as if my brain was evaporating."

"Jesus," Dorsett said.

" 'White Darkness' is a state of simultaneous ecstasy and terror. The drums transfixed me. I couldn't wrench my leg free. Something surged up my body into my head and overwhelmed me. I remember screaming *Erzulie*! Then I blacked out. I'm shivering just describing it to you."

Dorsett kissed Josi on the forehead. She clung to his arm.

"I'm happy you're in my life, Preston. Where did you make a hotel reservation?"

"At the Sunset Motel on Federal Highway."

Josi sat stiffly on the edge of her bench. She reddened as she asked, "Want company?"

He blinked with disbelief. "I registered with my Visa card. FBI male personnel are not encouraged to take beautiful female suspects into motel rooms. How about a moonlight stroll on the beach instead; let nature take its course?"

"No thanks. It looked romantic when Burt Lancaster and Deborah Kerr made love in the sand in *From Here to Eternity*, but trust me, friend, the sand gets into places you don't need to ask about. Besides, the tide's in. The motel sounds better."

"What the hell. I can always get a job as a history teacher."

Entering the motel room, they turned to each other. Their feverish bodies pressed close together. Josi parted her lips, sliding her hungry tongue in Dorsett's mouth. He pushed her toward the bed.

"Let's slow down, get comfortable and not ruin my only expensive dress," Josi said, giggling, going into the bathroom. "I'll just be a second. Don't start without me."

A few minutes later Dorsett gaped at the naked bronze goddess standing before the bed. "Do all FBI men get into bed with just their shorts on?" Josi teased.

"I don't know. I've never gone to bed with other FBI men."

"Right. You're from the post-Hoover era."

He inhaled her scent, sharp and tangy like lemons. Together they slipped into bed, warm skin on cool sheets. Preston touched her hair with his fingertips as her mouth slid down his stomach, and then he was lost. The rest was instinct, a craving. When he was inside her, she shuddered, her hips rising to take him, their bodies moving together slowly, then more quickly, as she moaned softly.

Afterwards, she lay against him until she fell asleep. It was close to two a.m. when a cellular phone shrilled from somewhere in their jumbled pile of clothing.

"Dorsett here," he stammered.

"Sorry to bother you so late, sir," the brisk voice apologized. "Standing orders are to contact you in the event of any incursion on the Treasure Coast."

"Okay, Martin. What's up?" he said, still groggy.

"Our people reported low orbit satellite images of Haitian refugees coming ashore about midnight on the beach near the nuclear power station on A1A. The sightings were clear enough to make out dozens of people crowding into a white U-Haul truck, headed north towards Fort Pierce. What do you want me to do?"

"I'll notify the Fort Pierce police. It's their turf."

Dorsett dialed another number.

"Hello, Chief Perini, this is Preston Dorsett. Yeah, you're in love, congratulations. That's partly why I called. Thirty Haitian refugees landed on Hutchinson Island tonight, sometime after midnight, and are headed in the direction of Fort Pierce.

"Do you record these conversations, Chief? No? That's good, because *you-know-who* and her daughter are most likely driving a white U-Haul truck. I'd advise you to notify the Coast Guard and go through official channels to buy some time. It's now two-fifteen. The Coast Guard won't get there for another hour. If you put up a chopper, have them check out the undeveloped beach area between the power plant south to Jensen Beach. By then our friends will be safely away. Keep your people off A1A until after three a.m. so they don't accidentally run into the truck. Just air and sea surveillance, and you're in the clear with no harm done. No, you don't owe me one. What?"

"I do owe you, Dorsett," Perini replied. "One hand washes the other, right? Your girlfriend, the Beauvoir girl, lied to us. She was in Guzman's apartment for well over an hour, not ten minutes, as she claimed. The ambulance arrived at 8:45, and the guard at the Ocean Village gatehouse clocked her in before he went off duty at 7:00. Guzman was her first customer. Now we're even. Goodnight."

Josi whispered, "Preston, I have a secret to tell you."

He reached for his clothes and managed a wry smile. "And I have one to tell you."

...22

"HOW COME YOU HERE, MAX? You got problems?" Tata grunted as she fumbled with the broken screen door latch. "Lawd. Everybody got problems." She invited him in, grumbling, "I know spirits want me to do healing, but it's a strain. Aw, don' mind this old woman, Max." The mambo's eyes twinkled. "How you like dat zozo herb?"

At first, Wolfe was confused. Then he remembered the sex potion Tata had given Millie. Embarrassed, he said quietly, "It didn't work for me. I rubbed it on, but the stuff smelled so bad my wife wouldn't get near me."

The old woman cackled. She leaned up against the windowsill and laughed until the tears came to her eyes. "No, man. You got to brew potion, make tea and drink—not rub on zozo." She wiped her eyes; her breathing was labored from laughing.

"Tata, I've come to pick up the Erzulie painting."

"Why you got do that?"

"It isn't safe for the painting to be kept in your house."

"*Tig vié min zong li pa vic,*" she said. "This tigress be old, but her claws never old."

Wolfe hesitated. "Tata, I know you poisoned Guzman with the zombie powder."

The old woman's dark, heavy-lidded eyes studied Wolfe. She shrugged and said, "When I was growing up, my mother know a whole lot about poison. I watch her and I learn what she tell me. She say, 'People 'fraid Voodoo cause we use poison against enemies. We use poison against French slave owners, we use poison against bad people. What else we got to use? You think the justice of the peace care? You think the *chef de section* want to help poor Haitian folks? Everybody try take something for hisself.'

"My mother be right. I believe in poison too. I believe in Voodoo,

135

the soul of my people. When you end Voodoo, we all be zombies. Poison been our weapon since Macandal, way back, and before, in Africa." She limped to the closet and solemnly handed Wolfe a wrapped package.

"Thank you," Wolfe said. "You're a good woman."

Tata watched Wolfe leave. She shook her head, muttering, "*Se bon ki rá*. Good is rare."

WOLFE FELT UNEASY with the valuable painting in his possession. He pulled off of A1A and parked under the shade of a large palm tree in an isolated area adjoining Fort Pierce Beach. Unwrapping the brown kraft paper covering, he gazed for a second time at Hyppolite's representation of his loa, Erzulie.

"So you're the black Marilyn Monroe," Wolfe said aloud, chuckling, as he studied the rose-colored doves flanking Erzulie's graceful body in the painting. Carefully he removed an X-acto knife from the glove compartment and made a thin surgical slit behind the painting through the top of the muslin backing. Reaching inside, Wolfe carefully extracted a yellowed, eight-by-ten-inch manila envelope. After scanning the contents, he muttered, "I'll be a son-of-a-bitch!"

Wolfe used his cell phone to contact Dr. Charles Basil in Haiti. "Call me, Charles. I need to talk to you right away. It's *urgent!*" Then he grimaced and phoned his daughter.

"HOW'S YOUR METER MAID JOB, Natalie Sue?" Wolfe asked. "Are you still under investigation for taking money from meters?"

"No, Daddy, Maynard paid off—"

"Don't tell me any more," Wolfe cut in. "Is your husband home?"

"Hi, Pops," Maynard's irritating, nasal voice answered.

"I've told you, Maynard, I hate when you call me Pops. You're almost my age."

"Sure thing, Max. What can I do for you?"

"I have a friend with the access code for a Bahamian bank account. He wants to remove the funds. Have you any experience in this area?"

"Why doesn't your friend just wire the bank for the money?"

"The original bank account owner died in 1971."

Maynard Greenbaum whistled, adding, "Interest alone will be heavy duty."

"Can you help me with this... situation?"

"Before I was indicted for insider trading, I warehoused *mucho dinero* in Nassau. If you got the account numbers and passwords, it's no problem—Pops."

"Thanks—*Son.*"

CONDITION YELLOW SECURITY was the announced state of heightened alert when Wolfe arrived at the airport. The President was flying to Palm Beach for a fundraiser. Wolfe was ordered to remove his shoes for inspection.

From a nearby office, two smiling customs officers escorted a shapely blonde.

"Dr. Wolfe, remember me, Jenine, the spa reflexologist? I was strip-searched," she replied, buttoning up her blouse.

"Aren't you supposed to be searched by a woman?"

"They said they're shorthanded," Jenine explained. "I'm on vacation from the spa, going to the Club Med in Nassau. This must be kismet, our being together on the same flight and all."

"Jenine, I'm flying to Nassau for the day, on business. I'm at least forty years older than you, and reasonably happily married. Besides that, you were going to testify against me."

"I have a confession to make," Jenine said as they sat together in the waiting area. "I took up reflexology because I have a foot fetish. Having a sexual partner with the right instep, phalanges, and metatarsals is psychologically necessary for my achieving vaginal orgasm—"

"Spare me the details," Wolfe interrupted her.

"When I first saw your tarsal bones at the spa and touched your flat feet with the sunken arches, it was an exciting sexual experience for me."

As they boarded the flight to Nassau, she whispered, "I've felt a lot of feet in my day. But, Dr. Wolfe, your instep is arousing and highly erotic, a foot-fetisher's dream."

"Thanks, Jenine. That really makes my day."

WOLFE TAXIED INTO NASSAU FROM THE AIRPORT. He reviewed his son-in-law's advice: "Offshore accounts are watched carefully," Maynard had warned. "Money is digital, and digital transactions leave tracks."

Following Maynard's precise instructions, Wolfe opened a personal account in Zugnisht Hentscher Ltd., one of the oldest Swiss private investment banks, located on Cumberland and Marlborough Streets in downtown Nassau. He deposited one thousand dollars U.S., in bills. Wolfe's picture was taken and pasted in a new passbook. Maynard had supplied the necessary letter of reference. Wolfe elected to maintain deposits in dollars and asked for no statements, which saved him from providing an address. He authorized the bank to debit his account twenty dollars U.S. The gracious young lady assisting him requested a code word.

"ERZULIE," Wolfe replied, feeling queasy.

The African-Bahamian bank assistant with a strong English drawl explained, "Normal banking services are available and wire transfers may be effected by facsimile or direct computer link with the bank."

Wolfe left the Zugnisht Hentscher Bank, reread his instructions, and walked up the street to the Royal Bank of the Bahamas, where he repeated the procedure.

Walking around in the blazing midday sun made Wolfe sweaty; his legs felt rubbery. In a small café he drained a cool beer. *Only one more step*, he thought, *then* qué sera sera.

On schedule, at one o'clock, Wolfe entered Credit Suisse, the quintessential Swiss bank, where François Duvalier's money was stored. Using the account numbers hidden for thirty years in the Erzulie painting, Wolfe deposited a thousand dollars in Duvalier's Swiss account. Before leaving, he asked, "What's the procedure for transferring funds by phone?"

The woman bank teller raised an eyebrow. "We require written instructions, including a handwritten signature or proper withdrawal code designation."

Boarding the five-thirty flight, Wolfe slept all the way back to the Palm Beach Airport. Then he drove south on I-95 to Boca Raton to meet with Maynard Greenbaum.

Maynard escorted his father-in-law into the extra bedroom that he used as an office. "Let's see if we have everything. Very good!"

Maynard sat at his computer and printed out a letter on official-looking Haitian government stationery.

TO: Credit Suisse Bank, Nassau, Bahamas
Please immediately wire-transfer the balance of account number 774398 to Zugnisht Hentscher, Final Credit Account Number 675-922.
Code designation: ERZULIE

Making certain that the message he was sending had no sender identification, Greenbaum fed the sheet into the fax machine.

"What do we do now?" Wolfe asked, his heart pounding.

"They will process it in the morning. Call Zugnisht Hentscher about ten o'clock and ask for your account balance. Just to be safe, wire transfer the entire amount into your account at Royal Bank, Bahamas, and call for confirmation a few hours later—then you're home free."

The following morning at ten o'clock, Wolfe telephoned the Zugnisht Hentscher branch bank in Nassau and gave the withdrawal code.

"ERZULIE," he said in a croaking whisper. "I'm checking on a wire transfer deposit to account 675-922."

Wolfe waited, gulping deep breaths to keep calm.

"Confirming your deposit, ERZULIE. Ten million, five hundred thirteen thousand, seventy-three dollars, U.S."

Reading from Maynard's instructions, he said to the bank operator, "I want to give you a further transfer of funds, to be confirmed by fax. To Royal Bank, Bahamas, Nassau, account number 434-989, ten million, U.S."

Maynard had advised Wolfe to leave something in the account to insure that the Zugnisht Hentscher branch would honor client confidentiality and protection from unwanted inquiries.

Wolfe was weary. Duvalier's millions were now safely transferred to his offshore Royal Bank account. How many laws had he broken? The thought of returning to the Florida penal system with Big Luther and his friends sent sweat trickling down Wolfe's side.

...23

THE VOICE ON THE ANSWERING MACHINE SAID, "Dr. Wolfe, this is Phillipe Louissant calling from Orlando. Preston Dorsett informed me that you are representing the estate in disposing of the Guzman Haitian art collection. Please contact me. The William L. Bryant Foundation may be interested in purchasing several of the works."

Wolfe dialed Louissant's Orlando number and was immediately put through.

"Thank you, sir, for returning my call. Two years ago, UCLA's Fowler Museum of Cultural History prepared an exhibit called Sacred Arts of Haitian Voodoo. This exhibit toured major museums in the country and was so popular that there's demand for a follow-up exhibition. Our Bryant Foundation, I'm proud to say, has been invited to organize the next one."

"That's nice."

"I understand that you are authorized to sell elements of Mr. Guzman's collection. If this is true, we are prepared to make an immediate purchase."

"What do you have in mind?"

"For the entire collection, I would have to discuss the prices with our board of directors, but I do have discretionary funding for opportunity purchases. I'm told the missing painting has been located, and it's an original Hyppolite of the loa Erzulie. I think this piece would add a decorative touch to our exhibit. What price do you have in mind?"

"I haven't contacted galleries or placed the painting on the Internet yet, but I have one bona fide offer for fifty thousand dollars for Hyppolite's Erzulie."

"From whom, may I ask?" Louissant said, in a skeptical voice.

"A Dr. Charles Basil requested the painting for his personal Haitian art collection. I can fax you a copy of his bid."

Louissant hesitated. "If I were to offer you seventy-five thousand dollars, Dr. Wolfe, are you prepared to conclude an immediate sale?"

"I would have to check with the estate's trustee, Miss Beauvoir, but I don't anticipate any problem in concluding the transaction."

"Is it in your possession?"

"Let's just say it's accessible," Wolfe said, feeling a familiar prickle of excitement. "I will be in Fort Pierce, at the home of Tata Beauvoir, tomorrow night at nine o'clock. They are having a Voodoo ceremony. If you're interested in picking up the painting, we could meet there. Her house is off of Avenue D at—"

"I'll find it," Louissant interrupted.

"I'm sure you will," Wolfe answered. "And please remember to bring a cashier's check for seventy-five thousand dollars payable to Josi Beauvoir."

...24

THE VOODOO CEREMONY PARTICIPANTS prowled around Tata's dining room table, which was laden with assorted liquors, cookies, candies, fresh fruit and flowers that gave off a thin, sweet smell. The centerpiece was a cake with frosted pink and blue icing, and letters that spelled, "Happy Birthday Erzulie." Wolfe also detected the pungent scents of basil, peppercorn, and peanut oil. He was offered thimbles of black, syrupy coffee. The crowd was Haitian plus a few Hispanic and black-faced guests. Wolfe was the only white person present.

Lionel Beauvoir approached. "Welcome, Dr. Wolfe." The houngan's handshake was cool and dry. Noticing the wrapped package under Wolfe's arm, Lionel asked, "Would you like me to store that parcel for you?"

"No thanks," Wolfe replied, munching on an apple. "Is this a regular event?"

"Every few months Tata holds a party in the basement room we use as a *hounfor*. Tonight the ceremony is to contact Erzulie and entice her to join the party and ride Tata."

"What do you mean, 'ride'?"

"In Voodoo, possession is communion with the spirits. If it works, Tata will transcend the mortal world and become the horse of the spirit. Her words and behavior will be those of the goddess Erzulie. The spirits talk plainly to the faithful, giving us answers to serious problems."

Wolfe tried to control himself from laughing.

Lionel ignored Wolfe's rudeness. "With Erzulie, you have to be careful."

"And why is that?"

"Most times, Tata gets ridden by Erzulie Frieda, the white goddess of feminine beauty. Sometimes the red-eyed loa, Erzulie Danto or

Ezili jé rouge, shows up. You can tell because she's got tensed muscles and clenched fists. A person possessed by Erzulie Danto can break out in an uncontrollable tantrum if the spirit is upset. *Ezili jé rouge* was the loa who fought with the slaves during the revolution and was slashed on her face. She can't talk. She just whispers 'da-da-da.' "

Wolfe stared at Lionel's clothing. "Isn't this some kind of a party? Why you are dressed in torn jeans and an old shirt missing buttons?"

"Meet Legba." Lionel chuckled. "In the Voodoo religion, the loa Legba appears as a feeble, ragged old man, moving painfully on a crutch. This conceals the fact that Legba is the most powerful of all the spirits, descended from the great Yoyuban spirit *Fa*, the god of fate. In tonight's ceremony, I will be Papa Legba. Every Voodoo ritual begins with a chanted invocation for Legba to 'open the gate' between the spiritual world and the physical one. Papa Legba's symbol is the cross."

"Is there a connection between Legba's cross and the cross of Jesus?"

"Two different worlds and two different symbols. The cross originated as an African symbol thousands of years ago, then it was probably taken by traders up the Nile and became the *ansate*, a cross shaped like a T with a loop at the top, used by ancient Egyptians as a symbol of life. For us, the cross represents the vital intersection between the two worlds, human and divine. We believe the crossroad to be a very dangerous place."

Wolfe followed Lionel down the narrow stairway to the basement.

"This is our peristil, the ceremonial space. In every Voodoo temple, there is a center-pole, called a *poteau mitan*, located in the center of the peristil. It reaches from the ceiling to the floor, from the divine dimension to the earthly world. That's how the loa descend, like firemen, from the heavens. Here we use the yellow chain instead of a center pole. It serves the same purpose."

Wolfe noticed Phillipe Louissant helping to seat an imperious-looking white-haired old woman covered in black from head to toe.

Her wizened face was the color of mahogany. The woman had long bony hands, with fingers curved like claws. Louissant's mother's eyes were hard, black and slanted. She coiled herself on her seat and glared in his direction.

An old man rushed up to Lionel, shaking with fear. He pointed to Louissant's mother. "I 'member that witch; she be Rosalie Leopold, the boss-woman of Duvalier's Macoutes."

Then the man eyed Wolfe suspiciously. "Why is this *blanc* here to listen to our words?"

Lionel put his arm gently around the man's shoulders and whispered in his ear, and together they walked away.

Wolfe sniffed the sour scent of cheap perfume. He turned to see two middle-aged women dressed in white, sitting on either side of a small altar, holding rattles with beads. The altar was a narrow six-foot sanctuary heaped with eclectic articles: a picture of a black saintly-looking mother and child, a colorfully-dressed doll, two daggers, a perfume bottle, containers of soft drinks and kleren, and two white porcelain skulls. Candles placed in deep glasses on the altar cast a pale yellow glow. A walking stick, with a head carved in the shape of a huge penis, leaned against the wall.

"What are the rattles for?" Wolfe asked one of the women.

They stared over his shoulders, unresponsive.

The altar candles flickered as a voice behind Wolfe said, "The women are holding *asons*."

Wolfe turned to see Phillipe Louissant smiling. "The asons are calabash rattles with beads; symbols of the Voodoo liturgy," Louissant said.

"And the skulls?"

"The skulls are not just scary old bones. They symbolize Haitian African ancestors, the cycles of life. Haitians say 'to forget one's ancestors is to be like a brook without a source or a tree without a root.' "

Pointing to the skulls, Wolfe remarked, "Are you going to feature Voodoo altars like this in your traveling museum exhibit?"

"The altar is an important part of any spiritually based Voodoo art exhibit. Ah, I see you have our painting. May I examine it?"

Wolfe unwrapped the picture and handed it to Louissant.

145

"Maitress Erzulie!" Louissant exclaimed, tilting his head in the dim light to look more closely. "The way she existed in Hyppolite's dreams, proud and vain. The ideal of femininity. Incredible! Notice the lushness of the setting. The three birds at her feet and crickets above, representing messengers sent by the male gods eager to court her, and the colors of the flowers complement her beauty. It's a masterpiece."

"My cashier's check, please."

"Here you are," Louissant said pleasantly. "Dr. Wolfe, Preston Dorsett speaks well of you. Perhaps someday we will be able to break bread together, and you can help me untie the Gordian knots of my life."

"You're an enigma to me, Phillipe: intelligent and personable, yet you're mixed up in—"

"I appreciate your candor," Louissant interrupted. "I wish things could be different." He continued to smile, but his voice had lost any lightness. "Dr. Wolfe, another proverb from my homeland says 'eggs have no business dancing with stones.' I'm afraid it's too late for me to change my dancing partners."

Wolfe thought about Louissant's words. Sometimes in the course of a session, a patient would say something that had an electric quality because there were flashes of understanding, insights of comprehension. These were moments any psychotherapist searched for.

"I would sincerely like to help you, Phillipe." Wolfe handed Louissant his card. "I'm retired, but I'm available for you anytime. Please call me."

Glancing across the room, Louissant laughed. "Mother wouldn't approve."

Wolfe thought, *Never take away anything from a patient if you have nothing better to offer*. He plunged in anyway. "Perhaps you let your mother influence you too much, Phillipe. She's just a person like you or me."

Louissant's face was etched with sadness and glistened with perspiration, causing him to look older than his years. "No, Dr. Wolfe, I'm afraid that she's not like you or me."

* * *

NEW ARRIVALS FILLED THE ROOM, overflowing onto the steps. The crowd, at first desultory, became more animated and started to chant:

"Fait un vever pou moin Atibo-Legba.
(Draw a vévé for me, Papa Legba.)
Atibo-Legba, l'uvri bayé pumwé, agoé!
(Atibon Legba, remove the barrier for me!)
Pu mwé pasé.
(So I may pass through.)
Lo m'a tuné, m'salié loa-yo.
(When I come back I will salute the loa.)
Vodu Legba, l'uvri hayé pu mwé.
(Vodoo Legba, remove the barrier for me.)"

Josi stood by Wolfe's side as Lionel Beauvoir entered the circle and lit a candle. He picked up a small amount of flour between his thumb and forefinger and let it sift to the floor, forming a vévé pattern for Erzulie in a lace-like, heart-shaped design of granules.

"The vévé for Erzulie," Josi explains, "depicts Erzulie Frieda's symbolic heart, but the dagger piercing it is a reminder of the violence and anger of the Petro spirit, Erzulie Danto. By creating the vévé, Legba is summoning the loa to leave the spiritual world and to appear to us through possession."

Tata moved into the center of the room, sitting on a low wooden stool. She opened a bottle of kleren, tipped it three times toward the yellow chain *piteau mitan*, and drank. A murmur of approval came from the audience. Tata made the sign of the cross and began to intone Catholic prayers. "Our Father who art in heaven—"

Everyone joined in as she led them in "Come, my God, come."

Tata completed the Hail Mary and Apostle's Creed, then paused for a glass of water. She picked up the ason, shook it, and sang in Creole, shifting from the solemn Catholic chanting to the cross-rhythms of Voodoo. Two musicians started beating polyphonic beats on their drums.

A tidal wave of sound rolled in over Tata's rapid chanting. People clapped to the beat. Tata reminded them who they were and where they came from. With each snap of her wrists the beads rattled in the ason.

"*Lafanmi sanble.* (The family is assembled.)
Sanble nan. (Gathered in.)
Se Kreyol nou ye. (We are Creoles.)
Pa genyen Ginen anko. (Who have Africa no longer.)"

With a steady, rhythmic clapping, the people sang together:

"*Depi anwo, jouk anba.* (From on high, right down below.)
Nan Ginen, tand la. (Africa listens.)
Mezanmi, tout sa m'ape fe-a (My friends, everything I am doing)
Nan Ginen tande (Is heard in Africa.)
Bo manman mwen. (The family of my mother.)
Bo papa mwe. (The family of my father.)
Nan Ginen tande. (In Africa, they hear.)"

The circle stretched wider. Another figure was admitted. Lionel Beauvoir reappeared, dressed as an old man hobbling on crutches. Raising one crutch, Beauvoir declared: "We have no father. We have no mother. We come out of Guinée, but we did not come out of Guinée because we wanted to."

The room was quiet as a tomb.

"Welcome Erzulie," Tata called out. "My house is your house. Me, I'm goin' do everything you want me to. When you tell me sit, I goin' sit. When you tell me jump, I goin' jump. When you tell me anything, I goin' do it. My house is for you." Tata faced her son Lionel and chanted:

"*Papa Legba, ouri barye-a.* (Papa Legba, open the gate.)
Ouvri barye Atibon (Open the gate, Atibon)
Pou nou pase la. (To let us come in.)"

Then Tata jumped to her feet, fingering her jewelry, swinging her hips and throwing saucy, ogling looks at the men. She began to dance. Women in the audience clapped their hands and rolled their hips in time with the drums. In spite of her age, her arthritis and her weight, Tata danced, hands on hips, shaking her shoulders with the rhythm, her pink silk skirt held high. Tata continued shaking, and after a brief period she appeared to be in a full trance. She was the loa Erzulie Frieda, speaking perfect French in a high-pitched voice.

Lionel rejoined Wolfe. The possessed Tata sang in a thin soprano voice:

"*Erzulie Banda, Erzulie banda* (Pretentious Erzulie, sexy Erzulie)
Erzulie Banda pase sa'lv (Sexy Erzulie outdoes herself)
Erzulie Banda, Erzulie banda (Strutting Erzulie, preening Erzulie)
Erzulie Banda pase ko-li (Preening Erzulie thinks she's something.)"

The power of the drum beats and vibrations changed from the Rada rhythm of one-two-three-pause, to a higher vibratory state, loud and filled with high energy. The beats increased in pitch, sharp like the cracking of a whip, reaching the sonic frequency of the brain's theta waves. Wolfe felt the deep, solid, relentless pounding of the drums vibrating throughout the room.

The drum sounds appeared to strike Tata in the back like deep, solid blows. With one foot rooted to the floor, she spun in a spasmodic pirouette. On the next wave of beats Erzulie Frieda was gone and the red-eyed spirit, Erzulie Danto, arrived. The irises of Tata's eyes moved under her eyelids. She raised her head, and specks of foam gathered at the corner of her mouth. Tata's eyes rolled back, and when they re-opened the irises were ringed with white, the fixed stare of the possessed.

Tata's body melted into the rhythm. She lost control, jerking and convulsing. She panted and sweated with a look of suffering on her face. Her fists clenched. "*Ezili jé rouge*," Tata intoned in Creole, "*Le ou we Danto pase, ou di se loray-o.*"

"What is she saying?" Wolfe asked, alarmed for the old woman.

"My mother is possessed by *Ezili jé rouge*," Lionel replied, a note of surprise detectable in his voice. "She said, 'When the red-eyed Erzulie Danto passes by, there will be a bad storm, and somebody's going to die.'"

The pounding drum beats continued.

Suddenly, Tata stopped twirling and stood still. She was staring at Louissant's mother, Madame Rosalie Léopold. Tata shrieked. The sound was the scream of the tortured, the bereaved, a terrifying, high-pitched, primordial moaning hiss. "Da-da-da." Then Tata pointed at Rosalie Léopold.

Wolfe watched in disbelief as a bright red scar appeared on Tata's cheek. The drums stopped. The room was hushed. Madame Léopold pressed her claw-like hands over her face where the skin stretched parchment-thin. Louissant hurried his mother up the crowded steps.

Lionel went to where his mother was swaying from side to side. From his closed fists he stuck out two thumbs and pressed hard against Tata's eye sockets. Her face was convulsed, her eyes shut tight. In less than a minute her trembling came to an end. Tata came out of the trance. Her knees were wobbly, but her strength returned, along with her presence of mind. She appeared exhausted.

Wolfe turned to Josi. "What the hell's going on?"

"Tonight's ceremony was to be in honor of Erzulie Frieda, the white Rada spirit, but grandmother's loa sensed a demonic presence in the room. Then Erzulie Danto, the dark Petro spirit, took over Tata's body and raged."

Tata slumped into a chair. She said, "I be gettin' too old for this spirit business, Max."

Wolfe remembered why he had come to Tata's tonight. "Josi," he said. "Here's your cashier's check for seventy-five thousand dollars for the Erzulie painting. It can't replace the loss of your mother, but maybe it will help you do what you really want to with your life—"

"*Whaaa-whaaaaaa-a-a-aark.*"A harsh screeching sound came from somewhere outside the house. Wolfe felt blood rush to his face.

There was a gasp from Josi. She, Lionel, and Tata exchanged worried looks. A low murmur, like an electric current, began to jump from person to person within the room, growing in volume until they heard a loud bolt of lightning and a rumble of thunder.

"Bad stuff happen tonight," Tata warned. "*Lé mal égzist!* The evil one exists. This not your business, Max. *Lé pié boue joué ek van, li pédu féy li.* The tree that plays with the big wind lose its leaves. You best to go home."

The wind was rising; the night was pitch-black, with no moon. Thunder clapped overhead. Clouds were illuminated by bursts of forked lightning. The wind hissed among the high leaves, snapping off twigs and small branches. Heavy raindrops, changing from vertical to horizontal, splattered on the windshield. Wolfe couldn't see the road. Trees were whipsawed into a frenzy as the howling winds merged with torrential rains, creating a violent maelstrom.

Another bolt of lightning cracked the sky. Wolfe made the turn from Seaward Drive onto A1A, driving through a river of rising water. He flipped on the radio to channel WQCS, 88.9 FM.

"This is a special weather bulletin and travelers' advisory. Sudden heavy rainfall, hail and a line of possible tornadoes are reported moving rapidly northwest through the Fort Pierce and North Central Orlando-Kissammee areas. People are advised to stay off the highways, except for emergency vehicles."

...25

"LOUISSANT IS DEAD," Chief Perini told Wolfe on the phone. "We got the news this morning. There was a car crash in Everglades Park near the town of Basinger. Motorcyclists spotted a car overturned in a canal. They called it in. The vehicle was registered to Phillipe Louissant."

Wolfe's chest tightened. "How did it happen?"

"Too early to know the details. My guess is that Louissant was driving towards Orlando. With the heavy rain and high winds, he probably missed the turnpike cutoff and continued on to the intersection where 68 dead-ends at 441—"

Wolfe cut in. "He died at a *crossroad*?"

"Intersection, crossroad, what the hell difference does it make?" Perini said curtly.

"What about his mother? She was with him last night."

"Only one body found, so far. I'm driving up." He paused. "Since you have so much interest in this investigation, I thought you might want to tag along?"

"GET IN," PERINI SAID as he fiddled with the dashboard knobs and cursed the tepid air that streamed through the vents. He adjusted the radio; background music crackled with a jangle of muted country-western sounds.

"Everybody lies," the police chief griped. "Defendants lie, witnesses lie, naturally the lawyers lie, bad guys lie, good guys lie— everybody lies." He paused. "So why did you lie?"

Wolfe felt an infinite weariness, aware that the police captain was waiting for a response.

153

"And while you're dreaming up an answer," Perini said abruptly, "please tell me why you secretly flew to the Bahamas last week." His flinty blue eyes turned and glared at Wolfe.

"I was afraid to tell you what I was doing. You might have screwed things up."

Perini's eyes narrowed. "Try me."

"When Papa Doc Duvalier was President of Haiti, he stole millions from the people; the money was stashed in a Nassau bank." He took a deep breath. "Duvalier's bank access code numbers were hidden in Guzman's painting of the black Voodoo goddess. For thirty years, Bernie had no idea the bank access code was wedged behind the painting he stole from Duvalier. Bernie was in the process of interviewing dealers to handle the sale. Somebody recognized the Erzulie painting and contacted Madame Léopold or her son. As head of his Tonton Macoutes, she knew exactly what was hidden in the painting. That's why Rachel Walters was murdered—"

"Now you have my undivided attention," he interrupted. "Go on."

"I borrowed the Erzulie painting from Josi Beauvoir, who as Guzman's heir is the legal owner, and removed Duvalier's codes. At Office Depot, I made a duplicate of the documents with phony access numbers. A local framer made the picture look untouched. Dorsett got Louissant to call me, and we agreed on a price to be paid in a cashier's check made out to Jossette Beauvoir."

"Very enterprising," Perini said, looking relieved. "Keep talking."

"I met Phillipe at Josi's grandmother's Voodoo ceremony and exchanged the painting for the cashier's check."

"What about Papa Doc's jackpot?"

"I asked my son-in-law, Maynard, to help me access and transfer the funds to a safe new account. The money is going to a hospital in Haiti. I was afraid if you knew about the money, you would feel legally obligated to report it. Then the politicians in both countries would fight over it in courts for years."

The car was halted by a state trooper directing traffic. Wolfe sniffed the swamp air; it smelled dank and humid. Behind jungle-like hardwood hummocks a black BMW was visible, overturned and partly submerged in the shallow water. Discordant ripples signaled the movement of alligators.

The tall Hispanic trooper approached. "Sir," he said, squinting in the hot sun, "the deceased must have climbed out of the car and wandered around dazed in the heavy fog at night. It ain't a pleasant sight. Take my word for it."

Wolfe exited the car and felt a blast of noonday heat. The trooper led them down a snakelike path through the savannas to a copse of trees. People were gathered around a dark form on the ground. The earth around the body had been flattened by the police on the scene.

"Over this way," the trooper said, leading the way with a heavy tread.

"Chief Perini!" said the medical examiner. "What brings you way up here?"

"Howdy, Sam. We think the dead man was involved in a case we're working."

Wolfe pushed his way through the cluster of police and park rangers ringing the body. He stopped beside a stand of tall grass and glimpsed something half unearthed and repulsively human: a bloody collarbone jutting from a bloated, twisted shoulder. Eyes and nose and lips and cheek, everything that was once Phillipe Louissant, was ripped and mangled. The ears were gone as well. Wolfe's eyes took in the pile of human wreckage, the jagged pieces of clothing that looked vaguely familiar, and the dried clots of blood. A gust of hot air rattled the high weeds.

The medical examiner explained, "The victim was first killed by wild pigs or hogs. Then the scavengers got to him afterwards. These pigs are becoming a danger to people living near the Avon Park Air Force Range. Even hunters tend to avoid the area after the incident last year when wild boars came after a local hunter. Even shooting half of them didn't stop the pack from devouring the poor guy before help arrived."

"There was a woman with Louissant," Perini said. "What happened to her?"

"The car is in the water with its doors open. Far as we know, gators could have got her."

The day's heat built steadily. Wolfe was sweating fiercely. He could feel his shirt sticking to his back as he moved around. The sudden horrific impact of eyeing Louissant's body made Wolfe sick in his gut. He staggered behind a bush and vomited.

A loud noise startled him from behind a bush nearby. He heard snapping and rustling sounds, followed by a cacophony of wild shrieks, crashing boughs, and agitated bird cries. Two heavy, grunting gray hogs burst out of the grassy savannas, humped up, with their salivating jaws thrusting, running in the opposite direction. The hogs were tracking something. Wolfe smelled a pungent flesh odor.

Black crows flew out of the palmetto thickets, crying shrilly. A large, eerie-looking bird, with a round head with tufted feathers, rose unsteadily out of the underbrush, unfurled its seven-foot long wingspan and soared away.

"Look at the size of that damned owl," a park ranger yelled, shooing the pigs away. "I never saw a horned owl that big before."

Wolfe's initial paralysis of fear was wearing off. "Can you tell me about the owl?" he asked the ranger, whose name was Politto.

"A fully grown horned owl is a terrifying creature, and among the most savage of the birds of prey. Sometimes it's called the devil-owl because of the way the hair tufts into what looks like horns. It's the only bird that can outfly a golden eagle. Its talons are as big as the paws of a baby mountain lion. Its loosely-packed feathers make it almost silent when it flies, kind of a stealth bomber of the night. This makes it easier to swoop down from the sky, stick its long sharp talons into a victim, and carry it off."

"Was this one a male or female?"

"Females are twenty percent larger, so I reckon it's a she."

"What does it eat?"

"Owls are meat-eating carnivores. Along with the bald eagle, peregrine falcon and red tail hawk, they're all raptors, or birds of prey—"

"What brings those ugly pigs here?" Perini interrupted.

"Housing developments keep going up near the air base in the Fort Drum area, disturbing the pigs' natural habitat. They'll eat anything from acorns to small mammals or any kind of flesh. If it's someone disabled and injured, they'll kill a human as well. The domestic pigs have black spots on white bodies. Now we're seeing new ones that look like razorbacks, with meaner dispositions and close-cropped gray hair. We call them hairless pigs."

Squinting in the hot sun, Wolfe mused, *Hairless pigs. Phillipe was eaten by cochon gris.*

The trooper called to Perini. "Chief, we've found something. It looks like human skin."

In the tall marsh grass near the palmetto thickets where the large owl had been spotted, Perini and Wolfe saw what appeared to be a small pile of dried skin tissue.

"There is an old Navaho superstition," Wolfe said with grim humor. "Witch owls leave behind their human skin when they change shape. If you pour salt into the skin and place it in a plastic bag, the witch can't get back into her body and she'll die."

"That's always nice to know," Perini said. "Let's find some shade. It's too damned hot."

"Chief Perini," the ranger shouted. "We found a package over by the puddle of skin. It's some kind of wrapped-up artwork."

DRIVING BACK TO FORT PIERCE, Perini reluctantly grinned. "You're not totally off the hook with your benefactor story. Both your sweet wife and the Beauvoir girl lied to me. Millie's fingerprints were all over Guzman's medicine cabinet. And the girl was in the apartment for a lot longer than she said. Care to comment?"

"Am I being officially interrogated?"

"We can go to my office. Have you heard of waterboarding?"

Wolfe raised both hands in mock surrender. "When Josi found Bernie on the floor in a coma, she was conflicted. Tata had seen the photo and told her Guzman was responsible for her mother's death. She hated the man, but he was her father. Josi panicked and called me, because I'm a doctor. Millie and I rushed up to the apartment. Bernie was on the floor in a stupor. His lips were intensely cyanotic; he was turning blue; his pupils were dilating, and he appeared to be paralyzed. His breathing was so severely diminished that there was nothing I could do. The man needed to be immediately hospitalized. I had Josi call 911. I told Millie to search his medicine chest for prescription pills, as I didn't know his medical condition. We left before the medics came. I didn't know Josi took the painting, but it doesn't matter. It's her property—"

Perini interrupted, "Remember what I told you driving up, about everybody lying?"

"Are you still busting my chops?"

"No. You're relatively harmless. From now on, steer clear of Dorsett. There is no Preston Dorsett who works for the FBI. I know you northerners think of us as hick cops, but we have our ways. I called a friend in the FBI's Miami Regional Office. He told me that agent Preston Dorsett was forced out the FBI three years ago on disability after being shot in a drug bust gone bad. They have no idea where he is. His mail is sent to a blind post office box in a little town called East Mims, Florida." Perini smirked. "And there never was a Eleventh Department handling expatriate Haitians. Our friend Preston Dorsett is a mysterious loose cannon working for I don't know who."

...26

SCHWEITZER HOSPITAL RECEIVES
$10 MILLION

WALL STREET JOURNAL. The Albert Schweitzer Hospital, at Deschapelles in Central Haiti, has announced the receipt of a $10 million grant from an anonymous donor. The trust fund will be administered by the Royal Bank of Nassau.

The hospital was founded by Larry and Gwen Mellon to provide treatment and public health in one of the poorest areas of Haiti, a community essentially without medical care.

Trustees for the fund are Dr. and Mrs. Charles Basil. Mrs. Basil, the former Inez Bunting, heads up the newly-formed Schweitzer Refugee Organization, providing legal aid and assistance to Haitians seeking immigration to the United States.

In a news interview, Dr. Basil announced, "This money gives us the opportunity to fulfill our mission of providing women's health services at the hospital and expanding to reach women of the Artibonite Valley with preventive care, health and family planning education, and better prenatal care."

When questioned about the source of new funding, Basil answered, "Haitians have a saying: '*Bon Dié di ou: Fé pa ou, Ma fé pa-M.*' God says, you do your part and I'll do mine."

* * *

"HELLO, MAX, THIS IS CHARLES BASIL. Sis and I want to personally thank you for your role in the anonymous largess we received."

Wolfe heard a flurry of hospital-like sounds in the background. "Thanks for the call, Charles. The local police are struggling with a missing person's case of a neighbor whom I examined after he collapsed. He exhibited diminished breathing, no pulse. I had him rushed to the hospital. They pronounced the man dead in the emergency room; he was buried, and then somehow was removed from the grave and vanished. It reminded me of the zombie you told me about."

"Clairvius Narcisse," Basil muttered. "Yes, it sounds familiar."

"I'm trying to be of assistance to the police. I know there is no scientific basis to zombies. More likely the condition is due to drugs or mental impairments, but—"

Basil interrupted. "Are you asking me if I believe zombies really exist?"

Sheepishly, Wolfe answered, "Yes, I am."

"As I mentioned at the spa, on one side you have the intellectuals, mulatto elite, and the Haitian government officials who have dogmatically consigned the phenomenon to fable."

Wolfe remained silent.

"On the other hand," Basil continued, "there are educated individuals—foreign and Haitian physicians and psychiatrists, in addition to writers and reporters—who claim at least some of the accounts are legitimate."

"Are there other cases you know about, beside Narcisse?"

"Not firsthand, but one case was reported by a woman with sterling credentials who lived in your town of Fort Pierce. Zora Neale Hurston was one of the preeminent African American writers of the twentieth century. Hurston reported in the early eighties about a young Cap Haitian boy who got in trouble with a girl and refused to accept responsibility for her pregnancy. When the girl's family approached his, they were turned away and offered no money, no anything.

"Two weeks afterward, the boy died suddenly and was buried.

Some months later the mother was wandering through the city when she saw some laborers loading ox carts with bags of coffee. In one of the faces she recognized her son. He stared, but did not recognize his mother. She ran for help, but by the time she returned, the foreman denied ever having seen the youth in question. She never saw her son again."

"You are hedging my question, Charles."

"My experience suggests that zombification exists as a form of social sanction imposed by secret societies as a means of maintaining order and control in rural Haitian communities."

"You referred to the use of poisons for zombification in your spa talk."

"Because of time constraints that evening, and also the sensitivity of older women in the audience, I brushed lightly the surface of zombie poisons. The potions contain a variety of toxic ingredients, and they fall into three broad categories. First, human remains, dried internal organs, shaving of skulls, and tibia are all included in every preparation."

"Go on," Wolfe encouraged him.

"Second, plants and animals known to be pharmacologically active are added. There is one consistent ingredient used that's found in various species of marine fish which contain in their viscera tetrotoxin, an extremely potent neurotoxin.

"Lastly, all preparations contain skin irritants—ground glass and plants with urticating trichomes, whose common name is the stinging nettle. If you touch it with your bare skin, it feels like a bee sting and is caused by formic acid, which covers the tiny hairs of the plant."

Wolfe said, "You're telling me you believe there is an ethnopharmacological basis to the zombie syndrome, and this poison preparation, whatever it is, can induce a state of peripheral paralysis, marked by imperceptibly low metabolic levels."

Basil sounded hesitant. "The poison preparation is only a part. It's not the poison alone that creates a zombie. I once cared for a houngan dying of prostate cancer. The old man did not wish to be doctored by a *blanc*, but his daughter, a graduate of the Faculté de Médecine, Université Notre Dame, in Port-au-Prince, was a general surgeon living in

Baltimore. The young woman flew down and insisted her father be admitted at once to our Albert Schweitzer Hospital.

"One night late I visited with the houngan in his room. We talked about a lot of things, and I asked him, as a Voodoo priest, what ingredients were in the zombie powder. He laughed at me and said, 'Doktor, you are not a fool, but as a *blanc* you cannot understand. You may gather your powders; in fact, I will give you all the powders you want. But you will never make a zombie—you do not have the magic.'

"Then the dying old man gave me the names of four preparations used to create zombies: *Tombé, Levé, Retiré Bon Ange,* and *Tué.* He refused to describe the specific formulae, but he did tell me that one killed immediately, another made the skin rot, and a third caused the victim to waste away slowly. He also commented that all of the virulent preparations had one ingredient in common—the *crapaud de mer,* taken from the puffer fish that I told you about. The old man whispered to me that that the best powders were made during the hot summer months, and then stored and distributed through the year. He said that telling me made no difference, because the powder alone does not work without the spells."

"So, bottom line, Charles, Narcisse was a zombie?"

"A few years after I last examined Clairvius Narcisse, I was made aware that he had been a pariah within his community. He was sentenced to zombification by the judicial process of the secret societies with their sanctions and their utilization of folk toxins and spells."

"Sorcery," Wolfe scoffed.

"Max, I have to get back to patients. Any houngan worthy of the name knows all the techniques of sorcery. Most consider black magic evil and have nothing to do with it. Voodoo priests take an oath upon initiation not to cause harm to others. The houngan only deviates from this line of conduct if it becomes necessary to protect someone he is responsible for or to lay low a criminal. If need be, a houngan can mutate into the dark Petro side of the loa Legba."

Wolfe felt his pulse racing. "I know a Legba who might have mutated."

...27

"LIONEL, THIS IS MAXWELL WOLFE," he said on his cell phone. "I'm in your neighborhood. Would it be okay to stop by for a few minutes?"

Beauvoir muffled the phone with his hand as he spoke to someone. "In about ten minutes, Max," Lionel said before hanging up.

Wolfe parked a few houses down from Beauvoir's driveway, hunching low to avoid being spotted if anyone looked out the window. He drummed his fingers on the wheel, glanced at his watch and peeked out of the window. Beauvoir's block was lined with modest, mostly well-kept, one-story ranchers. A few for-sale signs dotted the neighborhood, the windows of those homes boarded up, indicating foreclosure.

Old-growth orange trees and a huge, scarred elm shaded part of Beauvoir's front lawn. At the entrance was a multi-trunk jacaranda tree with green fernlike leaves and clustered lavender-blue flowers. Next to the jacaranda tree Wolfe eyed a large pot filled with strange-looking herbs and weeds.

The screen door opened. Wolfe was surprised to see Preston Dorsett standing with Lionel in the door frame. Dorsett's tie was loose, his suit jacket slung casually over his shoulder. Dorsett glanced up and down the street, adjusted his sunglasses, got into his car, and drove off, but not before Wolfe jotted down the license number.

Beauvoir flashed a smile in Wolfe's direction and waved a greeting. *So much for my surveillance career,* Wolfe reflected with amusement as he followed Lionel Beauvoir inside. The air conditioner in the window was silent.

"Whew. It's hot in here," Wolfe said. "Is your air conditioner working?"

Beauvoir picked up a small cylinder, misting the air over the snake's cage. "Da is shedding. I keep the humidity high so that his skin will come off in one piece."

Wolfe stared, transfixed, watching the python slithering against the tree branch, rubbing and pushing its nose on the rough wood, making a tear in its old skin. The snake lifted its head back, hissing softly. A layer of skin began to tear away. The animal slowly crawled out of its scaly covering, turning it inside out the same way a human takes off a sock—but in slow motion.

"Don't get too near the cage," Lionel cautioned. "African rock pythons tend to be more aggressive towards the end of the shedding. A film of liquid develops between the two layers of skin that makes it easier for snakes to cast their skins." He continued spraying. "This storage of fluid is the reason why Da's eyes are cloudy. Since this fluid temporarily decreases his ability to see, you must be careful. Da might accidentally strike out."

Wolfe edged back, his heart thumping rapidly.

"A python has strong instincts about food. Scent, movement, and warmth all denote a prey nearby. A hungry snake with clouded vision can easily mistake your hand for a live rat. If they get nervous you will hear a hissing sound, so you have a warning."

Watching the huge snake slither out of its old husk, Wolfe winced. He gazed at the dead eye caps and cloaca of the rolled-up, shed snakeskin. *Looks like a big condom*, he thought.

Lionel glanced at his watch. "You didn't come to see a snake shedding."

"I enjoyed the possession ceremony at Tata's," Wolfe said. "And seeing you as Legba."

Beauvoir's gaze was inscrutable. He remained silent.

"As a trained psychologist, I do not accept the validity of possession. It's been my experience that the seizing of the spirit of an individual by a supernatural entity—" He paused, trying to gauge the other man's reaction, then continued. "—with the result that the person's will is no longer free, but is controlled, by this indwelling power... Well, it seems to me that the participant must buy into this phenomena and is psychologically disposed to be hypnotized into a trance—"

Lionel drummed his right hand on the table, slowly increasing the tempo. *Whack!* His dark eyes flashed as he slammed an open palm down on the table. It sounded like a rifle shot. Wolfe was startled, but tried not to show it. *Whack! Whack!* The rapid staccato beat continued, repetitious, unlike any rhythm Wolfe had ever heard. The pounding sounded like cracking whips. Wolfe felt himself slipping out of control, his mind and body dizzily spinning around and around in time to the drum beats. He held his hands up in surrender. Abruptly the hypnotic table-pounding stopped.

"Did you believe that as an educated white man you were immune?"

Wolfe struggled to sound calm. Tension knotted his shoulders. He sank into silence.

"If my poor drumming offended you, I apologize. Please allow me to make amends by offering you coffee. Or do you prefer kleren?"

"Is the Pope Catholic? Kleren."

Lionel handed him a jelly jar half filled with the raw cane alcohol. They clicked glasses and drank, eyeing each other over the rims. "*Ayibobo,*" he said. "Hallelujah."

Wolfe sipped the kleren, reddened, then coughed deeply. His voice came out in a hoarse croak, followed by deep, wheezing breaths. At last, he was able to speak. "When you visited me in jail, you were adamant that in spite of the vévé scrawled on her wall, Rachel's murder was not caused by a Haitian secret society. And, as a houngan, you were in a *position* to know."

Wolfe felt the atmosphere suddenly charged with tension. He took a deep breath and continued. "I'm told that there really are secret Haitian societies that engage in vigilante justice."

Beauvoir shook his head. "It is only vigilante justice in the minds of people who believe rural Haitians haven't the right to police themselves or control their own lives. Haitian politicians have never provided basic services for the people. Do you know there is one policeman for more than 1,000 people? How is that protection? One judge for 200,000, one hospital bed for every 25,000. Our women carry food to market every day on rough roads. Who will protect them?"

Wolfe shrugged, but made no reply.

"Justice must be meted out by *traditional* means," Beauvoir said.

"And your secret societies are the traditional means?"

"Secret societies have flourished in Haiti since colonial times. Slave owners made an institution of cruelty. Field hands caught eating sugar cane were forced to wear tin muzzles while they worked. Runaways had their hamstrings sliced. Brandings, indiscriminate floggings, rape and killings were a matter of course, and for the slightest infraction, a man was hung from a nail driven through his ears. The death toll in some years rose over eighteen thousand.

"The societies at first were made up of escaped slaves. After independence in 1834, the function of those bands changed from fighting a hateful slave system to protecting their own community interests from inside and outside threats. Today, the societies operate wherever needed. They are the underground police force and tribunals that enforce the unwritten laws and prevent crime." Lionel's voice was dispassionate. "If we—if *they* find someone has committed a crime, the judgments are swift and severe." He glanced at the python. "Isn't that so, Da?" In response the snake cage rattled and the hissing sounded more pronounced.

Beauvoir continued, "Even today, anyone in the territory that the society controls can be brought to trial for violating the codes. The most serious punishment is zombification, or literally, expulsion from the community. Yes, this is a scary sentence, but you must bear in mind, Max, that the whole point of sanctions is that they should be truly frightening, or else the threat of them is meaningless. The society enforces a strict code of unwritten laws."

"Did Clairvius Narcisse violate the code?" Wolfe asked.

"Ah. You've heard about the zombie Narcisse. That man was no good. He fought with members of his family. He sired many children whom he didn't support, and he had a serious fight with his brother over land. He deserved to be punished."

"And did Bernard Guzman violate the code also?"

Lionel's smile faded. Wolfe felt the houngan's dark eyes bore into him.

Wolfe hesitated, then plowed in. "You are a houngan. You represent the loa Legba, who rules the crossroads and who knows all about zombie potions and powders and spells. Guzman violated the secret society code by causing your sister's death. In retribution, he was poisoned by your mother, raised from his grave, and resuscitated with the zombie cucumber or whatever the hell was used. Then you people let him go wandering off."

In a loose, shambling gait, Beauvoir moved towards the cage. He unlatched the top bar and, with a handkerchief in his hand, he reached inside. "If you grab a python's neck the wrong way," he said softly, "it can be risky. See how I throw my handkerchief over Da's head when I let him out. This alerts Da that it is not a feeding time and that I'm removing him from the cage." The twenty-foot python coiled slowly around the houngan's waist. "Once Da is out, I let him hold on to me as if I were a large tree. Notice how I support his head and neck with my hand." He advanced towards a sweating Wolfe. "Da is very intuitive and protective."

Max eyed the python uneasily. The giant snake's head was rising slowly in an S shape as it eyed Wolfe and flicked its forked tongue.

"For some reason, Da seems disturbed today and is hissing. In this world, Max, there are some questions that are best left unasked."

...28

THE FORT PIERCE POLICE STATION was located in the north end of town off of US1, a long, low, one-story brown brick structure with a forest of tall radio masts bolted to the roof. Stainless steel letters spelled out "Fort Pierce Police Department" over the entrance. Three flags flew briskly on the flagpole: the large American flag at the top; the Florida flag, with red diagonal stripes and state seal, in the center; and the smaller Fort Pierce flag at the bottom.

Chief Perini's sparsely furnished office was decorated with off-white walls, tough tan nylon carpet and steel filing cabinets. Reports and memoranda were tacked to a corkboard on the wall. Eastern light poured into the room from a window overlooking a golf course. Two visitor chairs covered in black micro suede faced the desk.

Sitting uncomfortably opposite the police chief, Norman Crabtree looked sad-faced and pale. The short, paunchy pest controller was close to tears.

"Better tell me the truth, Norman," Perini said in a bored voice. "You had motive, opportunity and means. Let's go with motive first. Your wife, Honey, was having an affair, and that made you angry. Right?"

Crabtree shrugged.

From gut instinct, based on years of observing body language, Perini knew Crabtree was not capable of killing anything but pests and termites. Nonetheless, he was required to follow up the loose ends. "Next is opportunity, Norman. You had a passkey to everyone's apartment. You were seen on the elevator the night before Guzman became ill. You are an expert in poisons—"

The pest controller interrupted, shaking his head in disbelief. Sweat beaded on his forehead. Crabtree reddened and inhaled deeply. "Honey and I are over. Kaput. She got a quickie Las Vegas divorce, and she's moved there. It's good riddance far as I'm concerned. Now

I'm free. I met a real nice Palm Beach lady who I greatly admire, and—"

"Chief," the switchboard operator cut in, "there's a Preston Dorsett here to see you."

"Send him in, Jessie." Turning to Crabtree, Perini extended his hand. "Congratulations, Norman," he said genially. "Love is a many-splendored thing."

"Huh?" Crabtree said, giving Perini a quizzical look and a wan smile.

Dorsett came in with a big grin, nodding to the departing pest controller. "Max copied down my license plate. Good work, Chief."

"Everybody lies," Perini muttered, gesturing for the man to have a seat. "Why can't I get used to it?" He reached into his top drawer and withdrew a micro cassette recorder. "Why don't we keep this chat on the record." A red light flashed on.

Dorsett leaned over the desk and flipped off the recording device. "I came in voluntarily. This conversation is classified information and officially off the record." He handed Perini an engraved card.

Preston Dorsett, Deputy CIO IT Security
NASA Security Operations Center (SOC)
300 E Street SW
Washington, DC 20024-3210
1-877-NASA-SEC
soc@nasa.gov

"Am I supposed to be impressed?" Perini sounded annoyed. "Is this your new persona?" Looking at the card, he pushed the intercom button. "Jessie, call 1-877-NASA-SEC and ask for a Preston Dorsett. He's supposed to be in Security Operations. If he's not there, leave a message."

"But, chief, isn't he in—"

"Just do it, damnit," Perini barked. Turning to Dorsett, he smirked. "What we have here, Mister whoever-you-are, is a question of jurisdiction. There is a missing person case in progress, and you have impeded the investigation by falsely—"

"Bullshit," Dorsett shot back. "I never interfered with your feeble efforts to find the wandering nutcase."

"Then why the elaborate cover-up?"

"How about some coffee?" Dorsett asked. "I'll fill you in."

"Jessie," Perini called again in a softened tone. "Any word on that call to NASA?"

"Yes sir," she said, sounding confused. "I left word with Mr. Dorsett's secretary. She will have him call you back as soon as he returns from... Fort Pierce."

"Thank you, Jessie. Could we please have two coffees sent in?"

Dorsett walked to the window overlooking the Indian Springs Golf Course. "This may sound farfetched, Dominick. And, if what I tell leaks out, of course you will have to die." He turned from the window and grinned. Then the smile vanished. "The government cannot afford this information to be picked up by the media—no way, no how. Understand?"

Perini shrugged his big shoulders.

"Have you heard of NASA's Constellation Program?" Without waiting for a response, Dorsett added, "It has to do with putting astronauts into space after the shuttle is retired. The program includes the Orion Crew Vehicle and the Ares I and Ares V rockets, which propel crews into orbit to the moon and beyond, both for exploration and permanent habitation."

Jesse came in with two styrofoam cups of coffee. "You two getting along okay?"

"Yes, Mother," Perini replied. After she left, he nodded for Dorsett to continue.

"During long missions, astronauts experience psychological and physical confinement. Data from the space station indicates that people isolated for long periods of time are subject to physical issues, depression, cabin fever, and other psychological problems. Naturally, this can negatively influence a mission's success."

Perini sipped his coffee, wondering where all this was leading.

Dorsett resumed, "Medical data from astronauts in orbits for long periods show adverse effects from a microgravity environment, in particular, loss of bone density, decreased muscle strength and endurance, postural instability, and reductions in aerobic capacity. Sometimes, astronauts lose up to twenty-five percent of their muscle mass on long-term flights. Those body motor disturbances only get worse the longer the exposure to little gravity, and they can affect operational activities. This is a big problem for NASA."

"Interesting," Perini said. "Are you getting to the good part soon?"

Dorsett paused, lowering his voice. "We know that human space flights are about to be launched by the Soyuz program of the Russian Federal Space Agency and the Shenzhou program conducted by the China National Space Administration."

Perini glanced at his watch. "I don't mean to be unpatriotic, but I have a department to run."

"Another minute or two and you'll get the picture. NASA has been researching these problems for years. We are working on a solution, but it's theoretical—suspended animation."

Perini looked puzzled. "You mean like the movie with the computer named Hal?"

"Right. *2001: A Space Odyssey*," Dorsett said. "Suspended animation is slowing the breathing, heartbeat and other involuntary functions without termination of life. Placing astronauts in suspended animation is currently under consideration for human interplanetary or interstellar travel."

Perini scowled. "Your two minutes are up."

Dorsett's voice was flat and uncompromising. "My assignment was to locate *alternative* and unorthodox anesthetic agents or psychoactive drugs for use in the space program. We can't go public and admit that NASA had serious interest in studying zombie-like powders to see if they could provide an answer to artificial hibernation.

"I was scheduled to fly to Haiti to secure samples of zombie powders, like the Harvard-trained ethnobotanist Wade Davis did in 1982. NASA wants a closer look at psychoactive drugs that can make a person insensible to pain and paralyzed, and the antidote which would harmlessly return him to normal consciousness. It could revolutionize space travel, and frankly, save the funding for our future manned space flights. When I heard news reports of a zombie nearby in Fort Pierce, I jumped on the opportunity to get involved."

"I can see it exposed on CNN," Perini laughed. "The astronauts' lawyers claiming they were victims of NASA zombie mind-control experiments."

"I know, I know, like *The Manchurian Candidate*. But this ain't the movies."

"Okay, Preston. I owe you one for your Hutchinson Island warning. Toots Bunting and I are keeping pretty steady company." He added, "What you've told me has nothing to do with my case, so there will be no leaks from my end. But, I have a question. Is that why you were visiting Lionel Beauvoir?"

Dorsett winked. "One of the reasons."

...29

MERRIWEATHER HEIR WEDS LOCAL PEST CONTROLLER

PALM BEACH POST. Mrs. Penelope Merriweather hosted a wedding reception at the Palm Beach Hotel on Saturday in honor of her granddaughter Babs' betrothal to Mr. Norman Crabtree of Hobe Sound.

As president of the End of Life Pest Control Company, Mr. Crabtree has received numerous awards from PETA (People for the Ethical Treatment of Animals). He is recognized as one of Florida's leading practitioners of helping insects die with dignity. Mr. Crabtree's practice includes termites, rodents, roaches, palmetto bugs, fleas, ticks, mosquitoes, and fire ants.

Among the honored guests were South Florida celebrities, billionaires, politicos, socialites, well-known sports figures, and exterminators from as far away as Jackson, Mississippi.

Immediately following the reception, the newlyweds, as guests of the Confederation of European Pest Controllers, flew to Europe for a sightseeing tour of the most historic pest control facilities on the Continent.

SEVENTY-THREE MILES NORTH of Palm Beach, at the Fig Leaf Nudist Colony, another wedding was in progress uniting the lawyer Pfarr and his betrothed, Wanda Smeltzer. A burly, bearded Fig Leaf Nudist Colony gatekeeper greeted the Wolfes, "Park anywhere. Take your clothes off, if you like, and follow the trail to your left."

"I'm certainly not taking my clothes off," Millie huffed.

Pfarr appeared on the makeshift wedding platform wearing only a formal black bow tie and loafers, his glossy black hair combed straight back. Wolfe was surprised to see so many of his neighbors in the buff.

"Ladies and gentlemen," Pfarr said to the assembled guests. "I would like to make a few announcements for everyone's comfort and safety and to avoid future litigation. The Fig Leaf's management recommends that all nude wedding guests avoid the surrounding barbed wire and poison ivy. Also, it is advisable to stand back from the hot grill while hamburgers and hot dogs are being charcoaled. Enjoy yourselves and have a wonderful afternoon."

Chief Perini, in full uniform, chatted with the Wolfes. He chuckled. "Toots wouldn't come. She hates anyplace where all the women are wearing the same thing."

Taking the chief aside, Wolfe said, "I'm meeting with the art dealer Valdesi tomorrow."

Perini patted Wolfe's shoulder. "As I told you, sometimes you have to let things go."

The all-nude male string quartet played the bridal march as Wanda waltzed down the aisle dressed only in a bridal veil and slippers. She carried a bouquet of *jasminium nudiflorum* crocuses, otherwise known as naked ladies. Wanda was joined by her nude husband-to-be at the altar.

Millie hissed, "Stop staring!"

Reverend Krumpholz joined the bridal party. He was a short, pudgy man with smooth, round cheeks and a fixed smile, resembling the late Jerry Falwell. Krumpholz was dressed in a natty blue polyester suit, yellow shirt, and a western bolo tie.

"Good afternoon, ladies and gentlemen," the reverend said. "God does not command us to wear clothing under all circumstances. The Almighty allows us clothing to help overcome our own shame in coming before him and before each other. How we clothe ourselves in any given situation should be governed by laws of love."

"What did he say?" Millie whispered.

Wolfe sighed and shook his head.

Krumpholz rambled on, "In Victorian times men were required to cover only their genitals and buttocks, but women had to hide their entire torsos and limbs behind layers of cloth. Indeed, the Victorian culture was so obsessed with exposed limbs that in a proper Victorian home, the legs of household furniture, which were considered part of the feminine sphere of influence, were covered with petticoats lest men would be moved to lust after the chairs."

"What is that idiot talking about?" Millie murmured.

Wolfe smiled. "Having sex with furniture."

"Now for the difficult question," the reverend continued. "Does the Bible prohibit Christians from participating in social nudism—"

Wanda tugged at Krumholtz's jacket. "Get on with the wedding, goddamnit!"

"Exactly!" the fat clergyman replied, averting his eyes from the bride's bountiful breasts. Krumpholz pronounced the marriage vows, uniting the couple in bonds of matrimony. Pfarr stood on his tiptoes, lifted Wanda's veil, and kissed her. The audience applauded.

Glancing around at all the lovely bare female bodies, Wolfe mused, "I wonder if there's going to be dancing?"

"In your dreams!" Millie responded. "We have made our obligatory appearance, and now we'll make our obligatory disappearance."

"Do you think it's the polite thing to do, leaving early?"

"Unless you want Elvar to handle our divorce, you better take me home."

"You say I never take you dancing—"

"In the car, Max. *Now!*"

...30

OVERHEAD FANS WHIRRED under the imitation thatched-roof ceiling. Vincent Valdesi entered Bahama Mama's Restaurant, spotting Wolfe sitting at the bar. Hundreds of caps, emblazoned with colorful emblems and logos, decorated the wall behind the bar. Wolfe led Valdesi to a table with a view of the Indian River. Children on the deck outside could be heard laughing as they tossed bread crumbs to swarming eddies of catfish.

A tired-looking waiter approached. "Ready to order?"

"What soups are specials today?" Wolfe asked.

"All we have is conch chowder," the waiter mumbled, yawning.

"I'll have the chowder, a plate of large stone crabs and slaw."

"Make it two," Valdesi told the waiter.

"I heard Phillipe Louissant was killed in a car crash," Valdesi said.

Wolfe nodded. "Phillipe's mother was with him in the car. She's still missing. Louissant left no will, and his employer, the Bryant Foundation, says they're unaware of any funds allocated for the Erzulie painting. The artwork has been returned to Guzman's daughter. I represent the young woman, Ms. Beauvoir. She's authorized me to dispose of the collection."

The waiter delivered two large bowls of chowder to the table. Wolfe added sherry to his soup. "I thought you might be interested in helping us market the collection."

Valdesi nodded. "I have connections here and abroad. I can get you top dollar."

"You must appreciate, Vincent, it's my responsibility to insure Miss Beauvoir is represented by an honest art dealer."

"What are you hinting at?"

"Valdesi isn't your real name, is it?"

"No big deal. Years ago I testified for the government in a drug case. They put me in the witness protection program. I needed a name that was suitable for a dealer in occult artifacts. Eight hundred years ago, a guy named Father Vincent Valdesius founded a cult of sorcerers in Europe. I liked the name."

"I think you know more about Rachel's murder than you've told the police."

Valdesi chuckled. "You asked me the same question when you were in my store. I've got an ironclad alibi, and you know it. So please let me enjoy this chowder."

"You're an expert on the occult, Vinnie. What's your take on zombification?"

He raised an eyebrow. "Don't tell me *you* believe in that crap?"

Wolfe shrugged. "You've just eaten the same chowder Tata fixed for Bernie Guzman the night he went diddy-wah-ditty. Yours was, shall we say, seasoned differently than mine."

"Nice try, pal."

"See the cook over there, Vinnie?"

Wolfe pointed to Tata, who waved back and gave him the thumbs-up sign.

"Poison is Haiti's weapon of choice. The cook is Tata Beauvoir. Bernie was responsible for her daughter's death. When she discovered that Guzman lived close by, she settled her debt."

"Bullshit!"

"If you don't believe me, believe your stomach. Soon you'll feel dizzy, and your breathing, digestion, and balance will be impaired. If you're lucky and get to a hospital, you might not die. But by then you'll be well on your way to becoming a zombie. Either way, you're about to join the cosmic world. And by the way—lunch is on me."

Valdesi wiped rivulets of sweat from his temple, frowned and pushed his plate away.

"Shall I continue?" Wolfe said. "I have the poison antidote, *datura stramonium*. Haitians call it the zombie cucumber. First, there's some information I need."

"You're out of your fucking mind, Wolfe."

"Why? It's the perfect murder weapon. No one found out what happened to Guzman. Lots of people ate conch chowder here that day. Good luck, Vinnie, or whatever your name is."

"*Wait*! *Wait*! My stomach feels funny."

"Were you in Rachel's room?"

Valdesi grasped his stomach tightly with both hands.

"Rachel and I both bid on Guzman's collection," he whispered. "I only wanted to handle the Hyppolite painting. Rachel wouldn't agree."

"Why only the Erzulie?"

"I'm sick!"

"Why only the Hyppolite painting and no other?"

"Last year, Phillipe Louissant contacted me looking for a Hyppolite painting called *Maitress Erzulie*. He offered five thousand dollars for locating the piece. When I spotted the painting in Guzman's apartment, I called him."

"Why was Rachel a threat to anyone?"

"All I know is she was going from the spa to pick up the painting and have it reframed."

"Who killed Rachel?"

Valdesi raised his voice. "I'm *dying*!" Diners at nearby tables looked over anxiously.

"No, you're not. Tata put magnesium citrate in your soup. You have a severe case of diarrhea. Go to the men's room, then we'll talk."

Valdesi rushed from the table.

Tata ambled over, wiping her hands on her apron. "Everything all right, Max?"

"Tata, what if I ditched my wife and you and I ran off together?"

Tata cackled. "Oldsters don't be youngsters no more."

Valdesi reappeared, tie askew and shirt untucked. "You're a miserable bastard, Wolfe."

"I'm doing you a favor, Vincent. Most people wouldn't understand, but you know about loup garous because of your interest in lycanthropy. Presuming at the time Rachel was murdered, you were in a bar with witnesses and Phillipe Louissant was teaching a class, who's left?"

Valdesi didn't reply. He got up from his chair in a hurry.

"Where are you going?"

"Back to the bathroom."

Wolfe ordered coffee and waited. "Feeling better?" he asked when Valdesi returned.

"No, but I've been thinking about what you said. The only person left is Louissant's mother. She's one scary bitch."

"Did you know Rachel was strangled? Her neck injuries resemble claw marks. A few minutes after Rachel was murdered, a large bird flew over my head on the beach, trailing light like a comet. It dripped blood on my shoulder."

Valdesi's eyes widened. "Jesus."

Wolfe continued. "Do you know that Mrs. Léopold's body wasn't found at the wreck? And I saw a huge female great horned owl fly away from Louissant's dead body."

"That's not proof, just superstitious guesswork."

"They found a pile of dried skin next to the painting. You know what that means?"

"Supposedly a loup garou shedding her skin."

"Vinnie, you and I are the only people who can connect Louissant's mother to the Erzulie painting and Rachel's murder. If she *is* a loup garou, your life is in danger."

"Not to worry. I'm headed to Haiti tomorrow for my six-month stint. I still would like to handle the sale of Guzman's paintings. Put in a good word for me? It's the very least you can do after literally scaring the shit out of me."

"Good luck, Vinnie. Be careful."

"You best be careful too, pal."

Before leaving, Wolfe went in the kitchen to say goodbye to Tata. The old Voodoo priestess wore an expression of sadness.

"Max, I got the bad feelin'." She closed her eyes and touched Wolfe's forehead with her brown, gnarled hands, murmuring an incantation. Then the mambo reached inside the pocket of her smock and withdrew a bright red scarf. She tied it around Wolfe's neck. "You wear this. Be strong like Ogou."

PART IV

DAMBALLAH

Dábala-wédo, papa
U kulév-o (You are a serpent)
Kulév, kulév-o (Serpent, serpent-o)
Nan fé brin pa bri rat (In the dark people afraid)
Atansion tig lé lougarou (Watch out for the werewolf)

...31

THIRD U. S. CITIZEN MURDERED
IN HAITI THIS YEAR

NEW YORK TIMES. Since March, three United States citizens have died in Haiti. Today, police reported the death of Palm Beach art dealer Vincent Valdesi.

In March, tourist Mary Hentscall was robbed and killed as she left an ATM machine in daylight. In May, Roberto Martinez was murdered in his jeep late at night on the outskirts of Port-au-Prince.

The strangled body of Vincent Valdesi was found in Petionville, a Port-au-Prince suburb. Robbery was ruled out. Valdesi's wallet and credit cards were untouched.

Haitian police were puzzled by deep claw marks found on the victim's neck as well as feathers discovered in the dead man's fist. A Voodoo houngan, Justin Desquiron, was called in by police to examine the feathers. The houngan declared the man had been killed by a demonic force called a loup garou.

Haitian government officials scoffed at Desquiron's comments, denying evidence of black magic or Voodoo. The official finding is that the murder was a retribution. Five years earlier, Valdesi had been a government witness in the trial of a Haitian drug dealer. Police are continuing their investigation.

..32

"YOU LIED TO ME," Josi said, a quiet edge to her voice. They sat on a bench in the waterfront park in Downtown Fort Pierce. Tears welled in her eyes. The glint of yellow lights from South Hutchinson Island reflected across the water. Josi studied Preston's graying temples and his strong, almost chiseled face. "In a way, I'm grateful. You helped me make a decision."

Dorsett sighed audibly. "I was on an important classified mission connected to the American space program—"

Josi cut in. "You used me to get close to Uncle Lionel."

Dorsett dismissed the barb. "Yes, I was trying to secure chemical powders to test for our long-range manned space program. It's vital that we find ways to keep astronauts functioning during long space flights—"

She interrupted again. "Unmanned flight is safer and cheaper, but not as glamorous. You NASA people push manned space flight because that gets the media's attention and keeps the money rolling in. Money that could be used for education, health care and helping poor people."

Dorsett nodded, not in agreement, but in his understanding of Josi's opinion. "Have you ever heard of Agent Orange?" he asked.

"The horrible chemical you people used in Vietnam."

He ignored the "you people" comment. "Agent Orange was used as a defoliant in the Vietnam War. Thousands of vets suffered from neurological problems, birth defects in children, and rare cancers. It was and is scandalous that our military experimented on soldiers and civilians without their informed consent. Can you begin to imagine the publicity and uproar that would follow the exposure of NASA considering zombie powders for astronauts?"

She smiled thinly, shaking her head.

"The talk shows would clobber us. It would kill the Constellation program and probably impact the next presidential race. I concocted the FBI cover story in order to keep NASA's identity a secret." His fingers grazed the nape of her neck.

Her eyes shut in response. "You didn't trust me," she whispered. "Haitians have a proverb: trust is like an icicle; once it melts, that's the end of it."

A trace of anger crept into his face. "My assignment concerned the national interests. I did what I had to do."

Josi moved closer so that their arms touched. She sat and looked at him. "I'm also doing what I have to do—moving to Haiti."

"I spoke to your uncle," he mumbled. "I asked his permission to marry you."

Without looking up at Preston, Josi slowly exhaled. "At this time, it is not possible. I've made a commitment to Voodoo. It's in my blood. Tata is getting older. I intend to follow in her steps and become a mambo."

"How long will you be gone?" Dorsett asked, a sickness rising in his gut.

"At least a year. It takes several weeks to complete the *kanzo* ritual. Then I will go to my mother's hometown, Ville-Bonheur, to assist the local houngan and continue my training."

He placed his hand behind her neck and drew her unresisting head close. He kissed her gently. Josi's mouth was soft and warm. He felt the smallest shudder of her body, and then, slowly, she ended the kiss. Softly, she said, "Goodbye, Preston."

..33

PANEL SAYS NASA ON UNSUSTAINABLE TRAJECTORY

NEW YORK TIMES. A blue-ribbon panel said Tuesday that a lack of financing and more serious, but unspecified, problems are seen as major constraints on NASA's plans for human space flight. With growing federal deficits and bruising battles over health care, it is unclear how much political capital the president might spend on expanding the budget for the space agency.

NASA, under its Constellation program, is developing a new rocket called Ares I and a new astronaut capsule called Orion. The system is scheduled to begin carrying astronauts to the International Space Station in March 2015. After that NASA had plans to develop a larger rocket, the Ares V, and a lunar lander, to lead to a return to the moon by 2020.

Beyond the question of rockets, an unnamed source reported, is one of human sustainability. The ultimate goal was Mars and beyond, but that is currently impractical. Alternative anesthetic agents that NASA was investigating to solve the problems of artificial hibernation, other than the unproved science of cryonics, have been dismissed as totally unacceptable by the blue-ribbon panel.

...34

COOAH, COO, COO, COOS. Wolfe sat on his balcony swatting no-seeums. He sipped a second Scotch and listened to the soft drawn-out calls, like laments, from a pair of slender-tailed, small-headed gray doves nesting under the thistle cactus plant on his deck. It was a starless night; the wind was rising off the ocean.

Wolfe's eyelids grew heavy. Dozing, he didn't hear the wild fluttering of little wings and the sharp, whinnying sounds as the startled doves disappeared from the balcony, flying away bullet-straight into the darkness. A large, tawny owl with tufts of feathers on its head like horns unfurled its seven-foot wings and landed without a sound on the deck railing.

Wolfe stirred, sniffing something musky and loathsome. Squinting in the darkness, he imagined he saw a huge animal with sleek russet feathers, baring its needle-sharp teeth and hissing like a cat. The raptor's slanted, menacing eyes were yellow with round black pupils. Then the creature emitted a snarl that shrank its yellow eyes to slits and cackled, sputtering in an unknown language.

Wolfe's mouth opened, but the scream was shocked out of him as the animal moved toward him. A sharp talon struck Wolfe in the face, knocking him backward. The pain was immediate and severe. The cords of his neck throbbed with tension. His nose was gushing blood; so were his neck and forehead. The breath was knocked out of him as the owl's sharp beak bit deep into his shoulder. His body shivered with the bronze smell of warm blood in his nose. Instinctively, Wolfe grabbed Tata's red cloth kerchief from his pocket to stanch the blood flow.

The moment he touched the red scarf, Wolfe heard loud drum beats, sharp as cracking whips. He felt a deep pounding in his brain and the tingle of painful needles in his neck and legs. A strange heaviness entered his body. He struggled against something invading his being. His foot rooted to the floor and he began to convulse rapidly—he was being possessed by a strong loa.

The fearsome owl poised to strike again.

In a trance, Wolfe cried out, "*Ogou! Ogou!*"

"By thunder I am here!" a deep-sounding voice roared. "*Lé-m kampé, la oué longé-m.* When I stand up, you'll see my height."

The malevolent loup garou, spitting with rage, attacked the warrior loa. They fought with feet and fists and claws and teeth, grunting and shouting. Ogou's hands shot out like pistons, crashing them on top of the creature's head. The owl's body quivered in a muscular spasm. The animal staggered, hooted, and flew unsteadily off the balcony. It hooted again, this time from a distance, and then a third screech sounded, *Whaaa whaaaaaa-a-a-aark.* While just as agonized as the first two, it was farther away.

"*Grains moin fret!*" Ogou roared. "My testicles are cold. I goin' home."

"MAX, MAX," MILLIE YELLED from the entranceway. "Where in the world are you? I called and called, then I carried up the groceries all by myself. I'm exhausted; my back is killing me. There's little I ask you to do around here," she complained, walking out on the balcony. "The least you could do— *My God!*" she screamed. "There's blood all over you."

Dark motes spun across Wolfe's vision as he awoke, confused, lying face down on the hard concrete balcony floor. He suffered dizziness trying to stand, staggered, felt himself sway, and eased down into a chair, pressing his hands to his stiff, aching right shoulder. He was damp with sweat. His shirt was ripped and wet with blood. Sweat glistened on Wolfe's forehead. Gingerly he touched his nose and right cheekbone with the tip of his index finger.

Millie tenderly wiped the blood from his face and neck. "What happened?"

"All I remember is having a nightmare about a monster owl. It was so realistic that to escape, I must have sleepwalked and stumbled into the cactus plants."

"Thank God you're okay," she said. "But where did you get that red *shmateh* scarf?"

...35

A MAN REEKING OF KLEREN entered the crowded emergency room of the Albert Schweitzer Hospital at Deschapelles in the Artibonite Valley of Haiti's Tenth Department. The bald, portly white man with rounded shoulders shuffled up to the Admitting desk.

"I know Papa Doc," the man mumbled.

"That's nice, but he's been dead for about forty years, old man," the triage admitting nurse said, eyeing his beard-stubbled face and faded yellow and green Bermuda shorts with drooping black socks—no shoes. "What is your name, sir?"

"Uh... Bernard... I think."

"*Mémous sé pasoue*," she said. "It's easy to forget things."

"They made me a *zombie*," the man uttered in a high nasal twang.

"Have a seat, Mr. Bernard. The doctor will get to you as soon as he can."

"I'm a condompresident," the man said, slurring his words. "I know Papa Doc—"

"Right. We already know that," the admitting nurse cut in. "And I'm Mother Teresa." She picked up the telephone. "Dr. Basil, we have a drunk and delusional patient here for the psychiatric ward. Please send someone down for him."

Whispering into the receiver, she added, *"Dokte, Pa okupé msié, kochon manjé santiman.* Doctor, this guy is hopeless."

...36

"YOU'RE GOING TO BECOME A WHAT?" Millie asked, putting her arms around Josi and hugging her.

"An *ounsi*," Josi said. "I've made a commitment to Voodoo, to become an initiate, and then someday, a mambo like Tata." She paused. "I'm leaving for Port-au-Prince on the 6:40 flight from Miami."

Wolfe narrowed his eyes and studied her for a moment. "Isn't this a little sudden?"

Josi's voice tightened. "No, not really. Several years ago, in a ceremony, I was 'ridden.' I was possessed by the spirit Erzulie. The experience was shocking—it terrified me. Uncle Lionel explained that this unexpected possession was a signal from my loa telling me to carry on the family tradition." With a tight smile, she added, "In Fort Pierce, our people are struggling with immigration, unemployment, foreclosures, and health problems. They are worried and are grasping for meaning and guidance. Tata says the Voodoo religion is the cement that binds our Haitian community."

"What kind of initiation do you have to undergo?" Millie asked.

"It's a grueling process called *Kanzo*, a rite of passage that transforms initiates like myself into devoted servants of the loa. The spiritual body of knowledge we will learn is called *konesans*. It's not written down anywhere, as Voodoo has no sacred texts, like the Bible. And you can't take an Internet course," she laughed.

"What are you doing with the Erzulie painting?" Wolfe asked.

"Tata's hanging it in our basement hounfor for a month, then Erzulie goes on display at the Vero Beach Museum of Art." Josi smiled. "Thanks to you, with the money I got for the painting, I don't have financial pressures, and I want to do something meaningful with my life."

"How does Preston feel about your going to Haiti alone?" Millie said, pouring coffee.

Josi made no answer; she gazed into her coffee cup. "Preston's not happy with my decision. I don't know how things will work out when I get back. I'm not going alone. Uncle Lionel is on vacation from his teaching job. As a houngan, he'll be my spiritual father."

"What's Lionel going to do with his pet snake?"

"Da will stay with Tata."

"How can a woman her age handle a twenty-foot python?"

Josi snickered and rolled her eyes. "Tata is a Voodoo priestess. Need I say more?"

Wolfe fixed her with a curious gaze. "I had a strange dream last night." He hesitated, "Don't laugh, but I think I was possessed by one of your spirits—Oguo. And I even remember the words he spoke: '*Grains moin fret.*'"

Josi laughed and clapped her hands.

"What does that mean?" Millie asked.

"It means," Josi translated, "his testicles are cold."

"Thank you for sharing that information with us, Max dear." Turning to Josi, she said, "The man scared me half to death. He was bleeding all over."

Wolfe said wearily, "As a doctor, I should have known better than to take my Diovan blood pressure pills on an empty stomach and then drink alcohol. My pressure dropped, and I must have experienced a vasovagal syncope. I fainted and fell into the cactus plants."

"Tell me about your dream," Josi persisted.

He hesitated, embarrassed. "More a nightmare than a dream. I was sitting on the balcony when a huge owl appeared out of nowhere. I could feel its hot breath, then the damn bird attacked me, scratching my face and biting my shoulder."

Josi paled.

"Then in my dream," Wolfe continued, "this Ogou character appears and chases away my nightmare owl. I woke up when I heard Millie's voice, then I showered and cleaned up the cuts with a topical corticosteroid."

After a short, awkward silence, Josi asked, "Max, did you say that the creature in your dreams bit you? And you thought the wound came from falling into cactus?"

Wolfe nodded, but remained silent.

"Were there visible cactus spines that you extracted from your shoulder?"

"No, but I don't get your point."

After some hesitation, Josi's voice became somber. "Please go and see Tata. Tell her what happened. She will give know what to do."

Her intensity surprised Wolfe. "I don't think I'll visit your grand-mother while she has Da as a houseguest," he said. "Snakes scare me too."

"I know you're not a believer in Haitian folk beliefs." She paused. "And I probably sound melodramatic to you. Maybe you were dream-ing, and maybe not. To some people, the bite of a loup garou, like the bite of a werewolf, is believed to cause dreadful consequences."

Wolfe chuckled dismissively. "I saw that old movie, *Franken-stein Meets the Wolf Man*, with Lon Chaney, Jr."

...37

IN THE STARLESS NIGHT, the loup garou hovered over Tata's house. The winged werewolf's black and yellow eyes blazed beneath her tufted brow. Short feathers on the raptor's face formed a groove, funneling sound waves. Alighting on the porch, the loup garou bobbed her head and snapped her beak, listening for sounds. The house was quiet. Tata was working, and Josi had left for Haiti.

The creature crept soundlessly through an open window and explored the stairway down to Tata's basement peristil. The owl-woman pushed aside the yellow chain *poteau mitan* in the center of the room —the pathway for loa spirits descending from the heavens.

Rosalie Léopold's pallid, ghostlike face leered as she spied the painting of Erzulie hanging on the wall next to the altar. She clawed the Hyppolite painting loose from the wall of the hounfor and ripped open the muslin backing, exposing its hidden compartment.

Something wild exploded in the darkness. A sudden rush of force struck the loup garou. Rosalie Léopold's shriek was part shock, part agony. Her hands clawed at the giant python. With heat sensors under the upper lip, the twenty-foot snake located his warm-blooded target and coiled around the writhing loup garou.

Rosalie Léopold uttered a strangled screech, burying her fangs in Da's glistening skin. Each time the trapped loup garou breathed out, the African rock python tightened its grip. Within minutes, the snake was wrapped around so tightly that breathing became impossible for its prey, and the lifeless bird stopped thrashing. The great horned owl's feathers were congealed in dark blood.

The python uncoiled itself and located the owl's head with its flickering tongue. The snake's loosely-hinged jaw stretched wide and began the slow business of ingesting the entire length of its prey.

Afterwards, a piercing, unintelligible hissing sound came from the yellow *poteau mitan* pathway that Voodoo spirits use to ascend back to the heavens. It was the sound of Damballah, the great African snake spirit. *Hsssssssssssss*!

...38

"PERINI'S NOT ANSWERING," Wolfe said, loading suitcases in the car, preparing to drive with Millie to visit their daughter Natalie Sue. "The Fort Pierce police say he's on leave."

"Toots called." Millie smiled. "They're fishing in the Bahamas. Did you cancel the newspaper, turn the air up and the put humidistat on?"

"Yes, dear."

"Did you close the shutters?"

"I forgot," Wolfe groused. "Get the mail while I do the shutters."

Inside the mailbox was a pristine white envelope addressed to Millicent Wolfe.

Dear Millicent:

I had the pleasure of meeting your friends, Mr. and Mrs. Pfarr on their honeymoon at the nude Orient Beach in St. Maartin. They related to me your exciting experiences with references to zombies and werewolves on the Treasure Coast. In today's competitive marketplace, vampire and werewolf books are the supernatural heavyweight genre. My agency believes your personal experiences lend themselves to a long overdue nonfiction book on the subject.

Harvard ethnobotanist Wade Davis in 1985 authored the hugely successful nonfiction book *The Serpent and the Rainbow* about how zombies do come back from the dead. Movie rights were purchased for the film of the same name, directed by Wes Craven, starring Bill Pullman and Paul Winfield.

We have discussed the project with a major publisher, who has expressed interest and proffered the attached check for $10,000 as an advance. Your job will be primarily to supply background information. Our creative writing team will do the rest. We would be pleased to represent you in this exciting project.

Most sincerely,

Sidney Skolnick, President

WOLFE FELT PECULIAR as he reentered the unit. His pulse was drumbeating and his head ached. He walked into the bathroom to take two Tylenol and studied himself in the mirror. Unless he was imagining it, his hair seemed thicker. *Must be the Finasteride*, he mused, knowing that the pill he took daily not only reduced the rate of prostate cancer, but also grew hair.

Suddenly Wolfe felt his teeth move in his jaw, and he experienced a sharp, burning pain in his hip, like something was breaking. He tried to open his mouth to scream, but his jaw muscles tensed; he was aware of his body jerking, contorting, bending itself into a different shape.

Beads of sweat dripped from his nose. He craved air, and half-walked, half-crawled towards the balcony as his bones arched and twisted. A change exploded out of him. Dark feathers burst from his hands and arms. Wolfe felt his spine contort, bowing his shoulders; his clothes began to rip. He realized with a flare of horror that he was sitting on haunches. His muscles throbbed from being stretched out of shape. His brain, his back, his tailbone all ached. He tried to stand; blood roared through his veins.

He sniffed. There was a strong musky smell in the air. His testicles had drawn up like hard stones and were covered with coarse feathers. His right ear rippled with pin pricks and began to change into a soft tuft. Wolfe's bladder let go, streaking yellow across the deck.

Through narrow-slitted, piercing yellow eyes, he watched in horror as his hands twisted into claws. He felt a terrible clenching around his skull and again opened his mouth to scream, but all that emitted was a shrill screech.

Most of Wolfe's head and face had already changed: the fingers and toes to sharp, deadly talons, teeth to raptor fangs, nose to beak. Slick with fluid, he jettisoned his skin. From the dark growth at the back of his spine issued two large wings.

The loup garou bobbed its head and snapped its beak, then gave a harsh whoop and launched itself over the balcony, leaving behind a pile of torn clothing and a small mound of wrinkled human skin.

CLOUDS THE COLOR OF PEWTER hovered over the ocean; a chilly breeze sweeping in from offshore. The western sun showed the last glint of pink against the night's dark blue sky. Seagulls circled above, crying restlessly.

Millie tucked the literary agent's letter and publisher's check into her purse and returned to the car, impatiently waiting to tell Max the exciting news. She was unaware that for a brief instant a burning, brownish, white streak forked crazily overhead, trailing a luminous comet-like reflection in the sky.

"Now where in the world has that man gotten to?" Millicent Wolfe grumbled, sniffing a damp, musty odor and feeling a vague un-easiness.

A spine-chilling screeching sound cut through the darkness, puncturing the silence over South Hutchinson Island like a death wail echoing ominously in the night air.

Whaaa whaaaaaa-a-a-aark.

Listing of Haitian Art

p. 10: Hector Hyppolite, *Maitresse Ezili*
        Musée d Art Haitian du College St. Pierre

p. 27: Loup Garou flag
        Private collection

p. 33: Hector Hyppolite, *Ogou on His Charger*
        Collection of Mr. and Mrs. Maurice C. Thompson

p. 34: Hector Hyppolite, *Les Zombis*
        Musée d Art Haitian du College St. Pierre

p. 34: Robert St. Bryce, *The Loas*
        Collection of Ned Hopkins

p. 36: Andre Pierre, *Three Loas*
        Collection of Astrid and Halvor Jaeger

p. 36: Rigaud Benoit, *Revenge*
        Collection of Gisela Fabian

p. 77: Dr. François L'Amerique Bellande, *The Demon Owl Woman*
        Collection of the Author

p. 109: George Liataud, *Zobop*
         Collection of Roy Pederson

p. 114: Paléus Vital, *Voodoo Ceremony*
         Collection of James Fastenrath

p. 115: Edgar Jean-Baptiste, *Phantom of the Night*
         Yale University Art Gallery
         Gift of Selden Rodman, B.A.1931

p. 116: Salnave Philippe-Auguste, *Anger*
         Collection of Mr. and Mrs. Harry L. Hughes

p. 118: Roger François, *Owl and Woman*
         Collection of Ned Hopkins

More from Chief Dominick Perini and the Fort Pierce Police Department! Please turn this page for a preview of

The Secret Diary of Marco Polo

A gripping novel full of action, intrigue and surprises.

A mysterious drowning in a Florida inlet uncovers a menacing international arms, drugs and oil conspiracy.

Available wherever books are sold
or visit www.malcolmmahr.com

ISBN 978-0-9825086-3-3

THE BODY BOBS FACE DOWN on the outgoing tide. At 6:14 a.m. the Fort Pierce Inlet is silent, except for waves persistently slapping against the rocks. The corpse floats on the surface, tethered by seaweed that restrains it from drifting out toward the freedom of the open waters of the Atlantic.

Two fishermen stroll along the concrete jetty, lugging their gear. The taller man, Walter, is a retired Army master sergeant with a dark, wrinkled face like an old walnut; his head is topped by a battered Army fatigue cap.

Walter spies an object floating in the water. "What's that—a manatee?"

His partner peers closer, then jumps back. "It's got clothes on, Walter."

"Holy shit! Use your cell, Jerry. Call 911."

"Police," Jerry mumbles into the phone. "A dead body's floating in the Fort Pierce Inlet, at Jetty Park."

At 7:05, Dominick Perini, the sixty-three-year-old captain of the Fort Pierce Detective Bureau, receives a call: "Captain, sorry to call you at home. We got a floater in the inlet."

"Great way to start the day," Perini growls. "Fill me in."

"A fisherman called 911. I dispatched two cars to Jetty Park."

Perini grimaces. He knows that the media will have a feeding frenzy over a dead body floating in the inlet. The news will probably make CNN, and the mayor and city manager will go ballistic; bad publicity scares away tourists, snowbirds and real estate investors. Perini takes pride in the fact that Fort Pierce's crime rate over the last two years has improved, but compared to posh Vero Beach to the north, and fast-growing Port St. Lucie to the south, Fort Pierce is still playing catch-up.

"Seal off the crime scene," Perini orders. "Notify Dr. Miriam Jolson. I want her to personally handle this case. I'm on my way. Tell our people not to let anyone near the body, understand?"

"Right, Captain."

The six-foot police captain dresses quickly. He catches his reflection in the mirror—flaring eyebrows, blue eyes, ruddy face, thick jaw, and bush of gray hair receding at the temples. He pats his growing stomach paunch and vows to go back to the gym on Indrio Road.

Aware that TV crews will be hovering around, Perini shaves in the car, a six-year-old navy blue Chevy Caprice with no police markings. When he crosses over the Indian River bridge to South Hutchinson Island, he has to shield his eyes from the brilliant early morning sun, rising above the orange-tinted, blue-gray clouds. Gentle winds fan the palm trees; gray pelicans drift lazily along the shoreline. Herring gulls swoop low over the mouth of the inlet, searching for breakfast. Dominick can hear the ocean, the rhythmic crashing and sucking of the water against the shore. Ahead he sees the flashing blue lights of patrol cars.

A crowd of fishermen, joggers, dog walkers, and immigrant construction workers gather on the corner of Seaway Drive and A1A— silent, just watching. Perini gestures to his officers to keep the people back. He asks, "Who found the body?"

The fisherman named Walter steps forward. "We spotted the poor bugger snagged on the rocks and hauled him out of the water."

"You should know better than to corrupt a crime scene," Perini grouses.

"Crime scene, my ass. There's sharks in the inlet, Captain. When that tide rolled back in, you'd have nothing but bones and rags."

"Sorry, fellow," Perini mutters. "You did the right thing. Give your name and address to one of the officers so we can get back to you." He turns his attention to the body of the victim, lying on his back, partly covered with a blanket. Perini observes that the old man is white, maybe pushing eighty. The face on the pavement, now an object of curious stares, is waxy and pallid, with receding white hair, a thin white line of a scar on his forehead, and glacier blue eyes staring vacantly at the sky.

Perini eyes the crowd. Two short, compact, dark-haired Hispanic-looking men in white painter's overalls furtively whisper together, then the men drift out of sight.

Dr. Miriam Jolson presses her way through the crowd and extends her hand to Perini. "Good morning, Captain—or maybe not so good, eh? What do we have?"

Perini smiles at the medical examiner. In her mid-forties, Miriam

Jolson is an attractive, fair-skinned lady, with copper-colored hair casually unkempt. Unmarried, Jolson has recently returned from serving a tour in Afghanistan as a captain in the Florida National Guard. The chief of detectives steps aside so that Jolson can examine the body.

"Fisherman found him," Perini comments. "Pulled him out before the tide rolled in."

The medical examiner scrutinizes the body carefully, making notes in a black leather book, then dons rubber gloves. She notes the victim's soaking and torn clothing: a short-sleeve, open-neck, patterned sport shirt and khaki-colored Bermuda shorts. His feet are bare. Jolson gently unbuttons the sopping wet shirt. Perini is impressed that the deceased is so well muscled for an old man. Purplish bruise marks cover his ribs.

"I don't want to corrupt the autopsy by poking around too much," Miriam Jolson says. "There are multiple scars on his arms and torso. Also bruised ribs, which might have been caused by falling on the jetty rocks."

The medical examiner pauses, touching Dominick's arm. "I don't know what's going on here." She lowers her voice. "Look at the obtuse position of the head. X-rays will be needed to confirm what I'm thinking—"

"Which is?"

"A broken neck. I think death was caused by having his neck snapped. I know it sounds barbaric, but that's the way it looks to me."

"Couldn't it be that the old guy broke his neck by accidentally falling on the rocks?"

Jolson takes out a small penlight and aims it at the victim's neck. "This man didn't accidentally fall. There's a suspicious perforation in the neck that might have been caused by a needle. If a tranquilizer was administered, chemicals may show up in the autopsy."

She removes from her kit an L-shaped ruler and camera.

"What's that?" Perini asks.

"In forensic odontology, when there is a suspicion of death or incapacitation by drugs being administered, we place an L-shaped ruler next to the entry hole and photograph it to scale. After the prints are developed, I'll take them to the pathologist."

Perini turns to his two officers. "You guys get busy. Canvas the area and see if anyone knows the victim or saw anything suspicious. The jetty lights are on all night, so you never know what you might find.

"Miriam," he says, "how long has the man been dead?"

"Hard to be accurate, not knowing how long the body was in the water. But there are lividity patterns on the body. Lividity is what happens to a person's blood after death. The heart stops, blood pressure collapses, and liquid blood pools by gravity into the lowest positioned part of the body. After about three hours you begin to see liverish purple stains."

"OK, so what does that tell us?"

"These purple marks aren't contusions from a fall. The victim was killed somewhere else, left lying on his stomach for a few hours, and then moved to the inlet during the early hours. The body hasn't been in the water long enough for serious deterioration to take place."

"This case is going to generate a lot of heat. How fast can we get autopsy results?"

"If they're not too backed up, I think the coroner could perform the autopsy this afternoon. You'll have results in the morning. Toxicology reports usually take two weeks, but I'm prepared to give you an educated guess. That anomaly in his neck is a pinhole with a slight bruise. I'd say your victim was first overpowered, tranquilized and then murdered.

"Let me get a few more photographs, fingerprints, a DNA sample, and a small slice of neck tissue for biopsy. Then you can call Tri-County and have the body taken to the new crime lab on the Indian River campus."

"Miriam, can you meet me for lunch at Bessie's Grill on Avenue D around one o'clock?"

"Of course. Why?"

"I need to review this case before I talk to Chief Thompkins. In forty years of police work, I've seen hundreds of dead bodies. This case is somehow different. I feel it in my bones."

Perini releases a long, weary sigh and takes a final look at the old man's thin hawk nose and his high cheekbones that suggest nobility.

Perini closes his eyes and pinches the skin at the bridge of his nose. Something niggles at him. It isn't specific. What he feels is an unexplainable sadness and melancholy in the presence of this victim. Something hovers on the tip of his consciousness, a resonant blank from somewhere.

LaVergne, TN USA
09 June 2010

185400LV00004B/22/P